CANAL WAL

SHORT CIRCU
ON THE CANALS OF
SOUTH YORKSHIRE

by
JOHN N. MERRILL

Maps and photographs by John N. Merrill.

a J.N.M. PUBLICATION

1990

a J.N.M. PUBLICATION,

J.N.M. PUBLICATIONS,
WINSTER,
MATLOCK,
DERBYSHIRE.
DE4 2DQ
☎ *Winster (062988) 454*
Fax: Winster (062988) 416

Conceived, edited, typeset, designed, paged, marketed and distributed by John N. Merrill.

© Text - John N. Merrill 1990.

© Maps and photographs - John N. Merrill 1990.

First Published - October 1990

ISBN 0 907496 65 2

Meticulous research has been undertaken to ensure that this publication is highly accurate at the time of going to press. The publishers, however, cannot be held responsible for alterations, errors or omissions, but they would welcome notification of such for future editions.

Typeset in - Bookman - bold, italic and plain 9pt and 18pt.

Printed by - Elgar Printing Ltd., Hereford.

Cover sketch - Croft Farm Bridge, Barnsley Canal by John Creber © J.N.M. PUBLICATIONS 1990.

An all British product.

ABOUT
JOHN N. MERRILL

John combines the characteristics and strength of a mountain climber with the stamina and athletic capabilities of a marathon runner. In this respect he is unique and has to his credit a whole string of remarkable long walks. He is without question the world's leading marathon walker.

Over the last fifteen years he has walked more than 100,000 miles and successfully completed ten walks of a least 1,000 miles or more. His six major walks in Great Britain are -

Hebridean Journey....... 1,003 miles.
Northern Isles Journey......913 miles.
Irish Island Journey ....1,578 miles.
Parkland Journey.......2,043 miles.
Land's End to John o' Groats.....1,608 miles.

and in 1978 he became the first person (permanent Guinness Book of Records entry) to walk the entire coastline of Britain - 6,824 miles in ten months.

In Europe he has walked across Austria - 712 miles - hiked the Tour of Mont Blanc, completed High Level Routes in the Dolomites and Italian Alps, and the GR20 route across Corsica in training! In 1982 he walked across Europe - 2,806 miles in 107 days - crossing seven countries, the Swiss and French Alps and the complete Pyrennean chain - the hardest and longest mountain walk in Europe, with more than 600,000 feet of ascent!

In America he used The Appalachian Trail - 2,200 miles - as a training walk, He has walked from Mexico to Canada via the Pacific Crest Trail in record time - 118 days for 2,700 miles. He has walked most of the Continental Divide Trail and much of New Mexico; his second home. In Canada he has walked the Rideau Trail - Kingston to Ottowa - 220 miles and The Bruce Trail - Tobermory to Niagara Falls - 460 miles.

In 1984 John set off from Virginia Beach on the Atlantic coast, and walked 4,226 miles without a rest day, across the width of America to Santa Cruz and San Francisco on the Pacific coast. His walk is unquestionably his greatest achievement, being, in modern history, the longest, hardest crossing of the U.S.A. in the shortest time - under six months (178 days). The direct distance is 2,800 miles.

Between major walks John is out training in his own area - The Peak District National Park. He has walked all of our National Trails many times - The Cleveland Way thirteen times and The Pennine Way four times in a year! He has been trekking in the Himalayas five times. He created more than a dozen challenge walks which have been used to raise more than £250,000 for charity. From his own walks he has raised over £100,000. He is author of more than one hundred walking guides; most of which he publishes himself, His book sales are in excess of 2 1/2 million, He has created many long distance walks including The Limey Way , The Peakland Way, Dark Peak Challenge walk, and Rivers' Way. He lectures extensively in Britain and America.

CONTENTS

INTRODUCTION

I started my canal walks in Derbyshire, a couple of miles from where I live. I never envisaged how interested and absorbing canal walking would be. With this book I have now walked more than 1,000 miles on the British Canals. So hooked have I become that I have had a narrowboat holiday and already booked another! On top of this I have explored the canals in Paris and followed the Rideau Canal in Southern Ontario, Canada, end to end - 220 miles.

Walking the canals of South Yorkshire is very different to my other canal guides because the navigitable canals are much wider for commercial traffic. Even so they still have the unique canal atmosphere. The other different facet is that the Barnsley Canal and the Dearne & Dove Canal are now almost gone.

To me this is a tragedy for a canal built nearly 200 years is part of our heritage and a monument of man's effort and determination. Tracing the Barnsley Canal has been a very rewarding experience. Here you step back in time and learn for yourself the beauty and majesty of the Canal era. Here man has dug, carved, built a canal through varying landscape for the betterment of others. To stand beneath an old bridge or find a pulley block or see the rope grooves cut into the bridge edges is to witness and feel a slice of history. This is why I have so enjoyed walking in South Yorkshire, discovering and learning what lay around the corner. The Barnsley Canal from central Barnsley to Low Barugh is a delight to explore. The section around Royston is outstanding and the final section just inside West Yorkshire between Cold Hiendley and Walton is by far the most exciting canal walk I have ever been on.

Of the bigger commercial canals, the New Junction Canal is fascinating; the Stainforth & Keadby Canal around Thorne is a joy to walk. The Sprotborough area of the River Don Navigation is equal to anything in Britain. For locks, the sad start of the Dearne & Dove Canal at Swinton is a magnificent relic. The Tinsley Flight on the Sheffield Canal is a rewarding walk and exploration.

Here then, are more than twenty walks on the Canals of South Yorkshire. I have quite simply enjoyed myself thoroughly exploring and getting to know the area more fully from a different perspective. Get your boots on and instead of heading for the hills explore this peaceful area it has much to offer , full of surprises and in 200 miles of walking I didn't see another walker!

HAPPY WALKING! *John N. Merrill.*

ABOUT THE WALKS

Whilst every care is taken detailing and describing the walks in this book, it should be borne in mind that the countryside changes by the seasons and the work of man. I have described the walks to the best of my ability, detailing what I have found on the walk in the way of stiles and signs. Obviously with the passage of time stiles become broken or replaced by a ladder stile or even a small gate. Signs too have a habit of being broken or pushed over. All the routes follow rights of way and only on rare occasions will you have to overcome obstacles in its path, such as a barbed wire fence or electric fence.

The seasons bring occasional problems whilst out walking which should also be borne in mind. In the height of summer paths become overgrown and you will have to fight your way through in a few places. In low lying areas the fields are often full of crops, and although the pathline goes straight across it may be more practical to walk round the field edge to get to the next stile or gate. In summer the ground is generally dry but in autumn and winter, especially because of our climate, the surface can be decidedly wet and slippery; sometimes even gluttonous mud!

These comments are part of countryside walking which help to make your walk more interesting or briefly frustrating. Standing in a farmyard up to your ankles in mud might not be funny at the time but upon reflection was one of the highlights of the walk!

The mileage for each walk is based on three calculations -

1. pedometer reading.
2. the route map measured on the map.
3. the time I took for the walk.

I believe the figure stated for each walk to be very accurate but we all walk differently and not always in a straight line! The time allowed for each walk is on the generous side and does not include pub stops etc. The figure is based on the fact that on average a person walks 2 1/2 miles an hours but less in hilly terrain.

THE SHEFFIELD CANAL AND SOUTH YORKSHIRE NAVIGATION

The River Don Navigation - In 1726 an Act was passed for improvements to the River Don to allow boats to reach the outskirts of Sheffield. In 1731 boats reached Aldewarke near Rotherham and by 1751 reached Tinsley. In 1793 two independent canals joined the navigation - the Dearne and Dove and the Stainforth and Keadby. The Barnsley Canal was privately owned. Boats were built beside the river at Masbrough, Warmsworth, Doncaster and Thorne. The latter was the biggest with boats upto 400 tons being constructed. The river gave access to Goole and Hull by linking into the River Trent. Further improvements were carried out and in 1821 to enable to handle bigger boats and more traffic an Act was passed and another in 1826 for bad stretches of the river to by passed by cuts, such as the Kilnhurst and Rotherham Cuts.

The Sheffield Canal - At first the Duke of Norfolk opposed the canal for a canal from Tinsley to Sheffield. Later he agreed to one on the south side of the River Don. This side made it easier to build a planned link to the Chesterfield Canal and Cromford Canal, neither of which were carried out. The Sheffield Canal Company was formed and was separate from the River Don Navigation company. The canal was authorised in 1815, was just under 4 miles long (6 km) and officially opened on February 22nd 1819. Considerable coal was carried with a 1 km branch at Darnall to link into a tramroad from the Duke of Norfolk's mine at Handsworth. The first large cutlery factory - Sheaf Works - was built in 1823 at the Sheffield Castle Basin. Today the canal remains as it was originally built with locks 61 feet, 6 inches long. Boats reaching Castle Basin can purchase a special stainless steel plaque. A small canal - Greasbrough Canal - was added near Rotherham (see separate section) but this was short lived.

The Sheffield and South Yorkshire Navigation was formed in 1888 and acquired the three waterways between the River Trent and Sheffield - Sheffield Canal, River Don and Stainforth & Keadby Canal. Also the Dearne & Dove Canal but the Barnsley Canal remained a private concern. The New Junction Canal was added in 1905 - see separate section. The section from Rotherham was classified as a commercial waterway in 1968 with 700 ton boats as standard to Rotherham. £16 million has been spent on the section between Rotherham and Bramwith improving the locks and bridges. Today about 5 million tons of goods are transported annually.

SHEFFIELD TO ROTHERHAM - 7 MILES

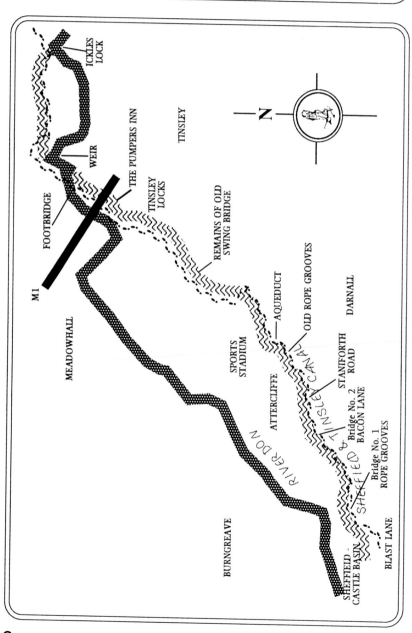

THE SHEFFIELD CANAL
SHEFFIELD TO ROTHERHAM
VIA THE TINSLEY LOCKS - 7 MILES
- ALLOW 2 1/2 hours.

 - Sheffield Canal Basin - Blast Lane - Sheffield Canal - Tinsley Locks - Ickles Lock - Rotherham.

 - O.S. 1:25,000 Pathfinder Series Sheet numbers -

- SK 28/38 - Sheffield
- SK 29/39 - Sheffield (North) and Stocksbridge
- SK 49/59 - Rotherham

- No official one but roadside parking on Blast Lane, a no through road.

- Plenty in Sheffield and Rotherham. Only one beside the canal at Tinsley Locks and reached via Sheffield Road - The Plumpers.

ABOUT THE WALK - A magnificent stretch of canal cutting through the centre of Sheffield and its industrial past. The canal basin is stunning and should be made into tremendous recreation centre! The canal passes many fine buildings and open countryside before reaching the impressive Tinsley flight of locks. Closeby is Meadowhall and the M1 viaduct. Beyond the locks and where the canal meets the River Don you cross a footbridge and continue by the river before following the canal to Ickles Lock. Here you leave the canal and walk into central Rotherham; you can follow the canal a short distance further but there is no way out! I have made it a one way walk as you can get a bus back to Sheffield, leaving a short walk back to Blast Lane. There is nothing to stop you walking back! As always the canal is a delightful haven in the midst of city life and industry.

WALKING INSTRUCTIONS - The actual canal basin is beside the major roundabout of the A630 (Rotherham/ M1) dual carriageway; just to the south is the Pond Street Bus Station. Access to the canal is along Blast lane, 1/4 mile from the basin via the first railway arch. You keep the canal on your left as you follow a well preserved section of canal and flagged towpath. You keep on the lefthand side for 2 1/2 miles to just past the Stadium built for the 1991 World Student games on your left. Here you cross over and keep the canal on your right and in 3/4 mile reach the start of the Tinsley Locks. A mile of locks - one blitzed on December 15th 1940 - and having passed under the M1 viaduct reach the end of canal. Here cross the footbridge over the River Don and walk beside the river on your right for 1/2 mile to where the river turns sharp right at a weir. Here you rejoin the canal and at first keep it on your right for a short distance before crossing a "foot-bridge" and keeping the canal on your left for the next mile to Ickles Lock. Here it is best to leave the canal and cross it and follow the roads into central Rotherham, using the prominent parish church spire to guide you. If you are returning the same way then simply retrace your steps rather than walk the 3/4 mile into Rotherham.

**SHEAF WORKS AND SHEFFIELD CANAL
AT SHEFFIELD CANAL BASIN.**

GREASBROUGH (PARK GATE) CANAL

Extremely little remains of this short canal - from Greasbrough to the River Don. John Varley, one of James Brindley's assistants, was commissioned in 1769 by the Marquess of Rockingham, to survey the route - 1 1/2 miles - but the plan with three locks was left to gather dust. John Smeaton surveyed the route in 1775 and estimated its cost at £5,952. In 1779 William Jessop began constructing the canal with four locks. The canal with tramroads linked the adjacent coal mines. In 1834, 10,452 tons of coal was transported on the canal to the River Don and Sheffield Canal , from Earl Fitzwilliam's Park Gate colliery. The boats could carry 30 tons and three worked as a train being pulled by one horse. In 1836 a railway line was built to the canal and as rail transport was cheaper the canal traffic was transferred to it; by 1840 it was disused.

BOATS PASSING THROUGH TINSLEY LOCKS.

KILNHURST CUT
- 6 MILES

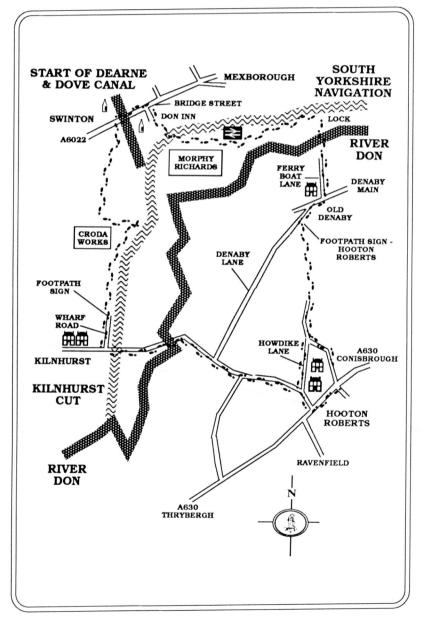

START OF DEARNE & DOVE CANAL

MEXBOROUGH

SOUTH YORKSHIRE NAVIGATION

SWINTON

BRIDGE STREET

DON INN

A6022

LOCK

RIVER DON

MORPHY RICHARDS

FERRY BOAT LANE

DENABY MAIN

OLD DENABY

CRODA WORKS

FOOTPATH SIGN - HOOTON ROBERTS

DENABY LANE

FOOTPATH SIGN

WHARF ROAD

KILNHURST

HOWDIKE LANE

A630 CONISBROUGH

KILNHURST CUT

HOOTON ROBERTS

RAVENFIELD

RIVER DON

N

A630 THRYBERGH

KILNHURST CUT - 6 miles
—allow 3 hours

—Kilnhurst—Kilnhurst Cut—Swinton Bridge— River Don— Mexborough Station—Old Denaby—Howdike Lane— Kilnhurst Road— Kilnhurst.

 —O.S. 1:50,000 Sheet No. 111—Sheffield & Doncaster area. —O.S. 1:25,000 Sheet No. SK 49/59—Rotherham.

—no official one.

Ship Inn, Kilnhurst; Don Inn, Ship Inn, The Towpath Inn, and Red House Inn, Swinton.

ABOUT THE WALK—When planning this walk I wanted to trace the start of the Dearne and Dove canal from near Swinton, but what looked feasible on the map proved awkward on the ground. This was due to the closure of one right of way which, although marked on the map, is now closed, resulting in me being bitten by a dog and charged by a very active horse! The delights of guidebook writing! However, I am pleased that I eventually sorted this walk out, for although partly in industrial areas it is very much a walk through history, seeing the Kilnhurst Cut, the abandoned canal and the old ferry point across the Don near Old Denaby. To complete the circuit a mile of road walking is required, and a small extension can be made to Hooton Roberts.

WALKING INSTRUCTIONS—I have started the walk at Wharf Road in Kilnhurst, on the Kilnhurst Cut. Here the B6090 road crosses the cut beside the aptly named Ship Inn. Walk northwards along Wharf Road to the path sign. Here continue ahead on the path beside the cut and keep on this for the next 1/2 mile to the Croda Works on your left. Keep ahead to a bridge over the cut and pass under it before turning left to the Croda Works road—the right of way ahead is closed. Bear right along the road to the railway bridge but turn right before it onto the fenced path and follow this round to Broomville Street and the beginning of the Dearne & Dove canal. Turn left up the street to the A6022 road and the perfectly named Towpath Inn.

Turn right along Bridge Street and past the Don Inn. Just afterwards turn right down New Street and cross the footbridge over the Kilnhurst Cut. Ahead is the Morphy Richards works. Turn left to the road and right along it. Where it turns right leave it and head for the stile with the Yorkshire Water Authority plant on your right. The path is defined as you make your way to the banks of the River Don. Keep on the bank as you follow it round for the next 1/2 mile before passing through a tunnel and gaining Mexborough Station on your left. Turn left then right and reach the towpath and turn right along it. 1/2 mile later gain Mexborough Lock and turn right, passing the Boat Stone and the footbridge over the River Don. Continue ahead along Ferry Boat Lane into Old Denaby. Turn right and follow the road for just over 1/4 mile out of the village to Lynfred Cottage. Here turn left as footpath signed—"Hooton Roberts", and follow the track southwards. After 3/4 mile and now on a tarmaced surface the lane forks. The left branch leads to Hooton Roberts. Ahead is your route along Howdike Lane to the B6090 road. Turn right along this, Kilnhurst Road, and follow it hack to Kilnhurst, crossing the river Don before passing the Ship Inn and regaining Wharf Road.

BAR G INN SIGN - SWINTON.

**SWINTON LOCKS - THE START OF
THE DEARNE & DOVE CANAL.**

MEXBOROUGH NEW CUT
- 4 MILES

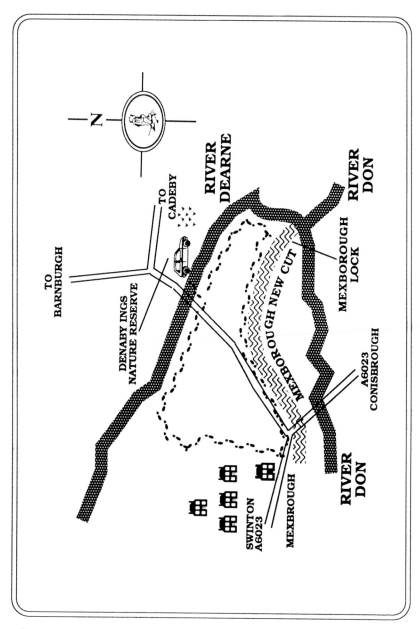

MEXBOROUGH NEW CUT
- 4 miles
- allow 1 1/2 hours.

 *Denaby Ings Car Park - River Dearne - Mexborough - Mexborough New Cut - Mouth of River Dearne - Denaby Ings car park.*

 · O.S. 1:25,000 Pathfinder Series Sheet No. SE 40/50 - Doncaster and Dearne.

 Denaby Ings Nature Reserve. Grid Ref. SE498008.

Miner's Arms, Mexborough.

ABOUT THE WALK - A short but very attractive canal and river walk. First you walk above the River Dearne before crossing fields and skirting Mexborough's eastern edge to reach the Mexborough New Cut of the River Don Navigation. Walking beside the wide canal you follow the "towpath" road to Mexborough Low loch. Shortly after is the River Don and the mouth of the River Dearne. You return above the Dearne. The start of the walk is from the Denaby Ings Nature Reserve car park, run by the Yorkshire Wildlife Trust. While here it is well worth while calling at their visitor's centre and also seeing how many birds you can spot.

WALKING INSTRUCTIONS - Turn left out of the car park along the Mexborough road and immediately after crossing the road bridge over the River Dearne, turn right through the metal stile. On your left is the stile which you will be using on your return. Walk along the path along the top of the dyke with the River Dearne below you on your right; keep on this path for almost 3/4 mile to the next stile. Here turn left to a metal stile and follow the path up the fields towards the houses of Mexborough. The path soon reaches the houses and you keep straight ahead on the fenced path, crossing an estate road on the way. The path later descends to a road. Walk down the road a short distance and turn left along James Street. Follow the road

17

round to your right to the A6023 Conisbrough road; to your right is the Miner's Arms.

Turn left along the road and in a few yards turn left onto the minor road to High Melton. Almost immediately turn right and gain the path along the Mexborough New Cut. The path is only short one before gaining the tarmaced drive to Mexborough Low loch. Follow this with the canal on your right. At the entrance to the loch - after 3/4 mile - turn left at the gate, as footpath signed and cross a footbridge and turn right. Follow the path past the loch complex towards the mouth of the River Dearne. Here above it the path turns left and keeps well above the river - I have seen mute swans, moorhens and a kingfisher here - as you curve round back to the road bridge you crossed at the beginning, 3/4 mile away. At the road turn right back to car park. Here a flight of steps leads up to the visitor's centre.

**BRITISH WATERWAYS REPAIR YARD
AT SWINTON.**

BOATS ON RIVER DON, Nr. SWINTON.

**FOOTBRIDGE OVER RIVER DON AT JUNCTION OF THE
SHEFFIELD CANAL (TINSLEY LOCKS) AND RIVER.**

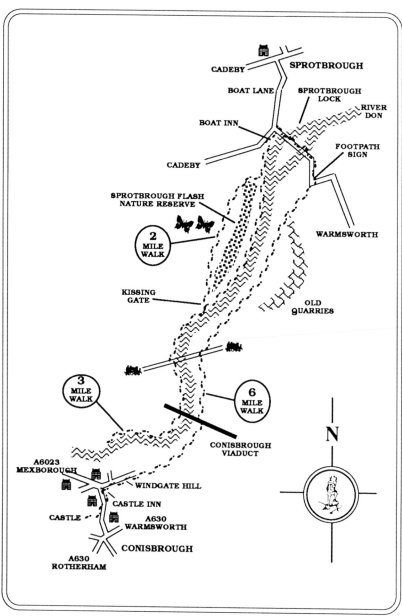

CADEBY

SPROTBROUGH

BOAT LANE

SPROTBROUGH LOCK

RIVER DON

BOAT INN

FOOTPATH SIGN

CADEBY

SPROTBROUGH FLASH NATURE RESERVE

WARMSWORTH

2 MILE WALK

KISSING GATE

OLD QUARRIES

3 MILE WALK

6 MILE WALK

N

CONISBROUGH VIADUCT

A6023 MEXBOROUGH

WINDGATE HILL

CASTLE INN

CASTLE

A630 WARMSWORTH

CONISBROUGH

A630 ROTHERHAM

RIVER DON NAVIGATION
SPROTBROUGH AND CONISBROUGH CASTLE—3 WALKS
—2, 3 and 6 miles long
—allow 1, 1 1/2 and 3 hours

—*O.S. I:50,000 Landranger Series—Sheet No. 111—Sheffield & Doncaster area*
—*O.S. 1:25,000 Pathfinder Series—Sheet No. SK 49/59—Rotherham Sheet No. SE 40/50—Doncaster & Dearne*

—*Near Sprotbrough Lock and Conisbrough Castle.*

🍺 *- Boat Inn, Sprotbrough and Castle Inn, Conisbrough.*

ABOUT THE WALKS—My original aim had been to have a circular walk from Sprotbrough along the River Don to Conisbrough and back along the other side of the river. Alas, in practice this is not possible as there is no way across the river on foot. As a result you have a choice of routes—one encircling the Sprotbrough Flash Nature Reserve; one along the western bank of the River Don to opposite Conisbrough and Castle; and the third along the eastern bank to Conisbrough Castle, returning the same way. All three explore a major section of the navigable River Don, with the Sprotbrough Lock nearby detailed in the Cusworth Hall walk from here.

WALKING INSTRUCTIONS—

2 MILE WALK—Sprotbrough Flash Nature Reserve. From Boat Lane in Sprotbrough walk along the towpath past the Boat Inn and along the well-used path with the Nature Reserve and hides on your right. After a mile the path swings right away from the river, with a kissing gate on your left. Keep on the path through the trees, and soon gain a walled track with the woodland on your left and views to the Flash on your right. Upon gaining the minor road, turn right passing the Boat Inn on your right.

3 MILE WALK—Basically the same as the 2-mile one beside the River Don to the kissing gate. Instead of turning right on the path, go through the gate and continue beside the river for the next couple of miles until you are opposite Conisbrough and its Castle. Here the right of way ends, and you will have to return the same way back to Sprotbrough and the Boat Inn.

6 MILE WALK—3 miles one way—Cross the bridge over the River Don and navigable section. Follow the road round to your right, and where it turns sharp left keep ahead on a track. On your right is the River Don and abandoned quarries on your left. After a mile keep to the path and through the trees, and follow it for the next 11/2 miles to the houses on the edge of Conisbrough and Windgate Hill road. Descend this to the Castle Inn on your left. Turn left past the Inn, ascending the path to the A6023 road. Just ahead to your right is the path and minor road to the impressive Castle. Return the same way back to Sprotbrough.

CONISBROUGH CASTLE - Earthworks date back to the 9th century, but the present circular keep and walls were built in late 12th century by Hamelin Plantagent, the half brother of Henry 11. The keep is one of the finest in Britain, with splayed base, six wedge shaped turrets, and walls fifteen feet thick. In the 15th century it was little used and in 1538 a considerable portion had fallen down. The castle has been immortalised in Sir Walter Scott's novel, Ivanhoe.

RIVER DON & SPROTBROUGH LOCK.

THE BOAT INN, SPROTBROUGH.

SPROTBROUGH & CUSWORTH HALL - 7 MILES

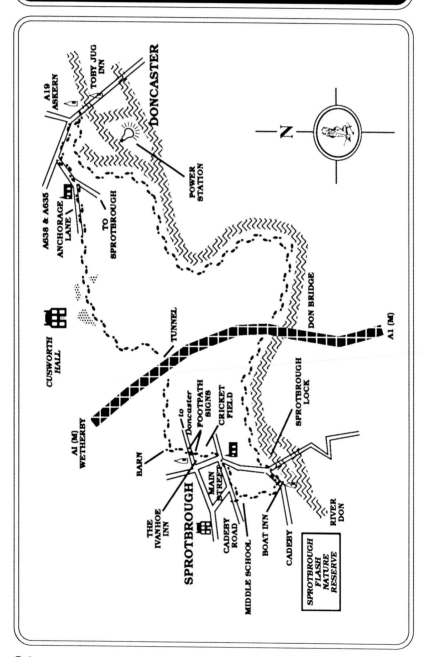

—Sprotbrough Bridge—River Don—A635, St. Mary's Bridge—Cusworth Hall—A1—Sprotbrough—Sprotbrough Bridge.

 —O.S. 1:50,000 Landranger Series—Sheet No. 111—Sheffield & Doncaster area.
O.S. 1:25,000 Pathfinder Series—Sheet No. SE 40/50— Doncaster & Dearne.

—Near Sprotbrough Bridge and Cusworth Hall.

- The Boat Inn, Sprotbrough; Toby Jug Inn and Three Horse Shoes Inn, Doncaster.

ABOUT THE WALK—The first half of the walk is along the banks of the River Don into the heart of Doncaster. You return to Sprotbrough along well-defined paths past Cusworth Hall, where a side trip can be taken to visit the Hall and Museum. After passing under the A1 you reach Sprotbrough, a particularly interesting village, before descending to the Boat Inn and the River Don.

WALKING INSTRUCTIONS—From Sprotbrough Bridge descend to the River Don and the canal cut. Turn left and pass under the bridge and on past Sprotbrough Lock. Shortly afterwards pass the remains of a waterwheel on your left, which fed water to the now demolished Sprotbrough Hall. Keep on the defined path for the next three miles, with the River Don on your right . Pass under Don Bridge (A 1), and 2 miles later keep right past a farm and buildings on your left. Basically keep to the bank top and you will reach all the stiles. A little over 1/4 mile later reach a side channel with a bridge across. Don't cross this, but turn left along the banks keeping the side channel on your right. 3/4 mile later gain the A635 road in Doncaster opposite the Three Horse Shoes Inn.

Turn left to the roundabout, and basically keep ahead on the A635 following the signs to Sprotbrough. Pass under the railway bridge, and almost immediately afterwards turn left into Sprotbrough Road. After 1/4 mile and where the road bears left, turn right into Anchorage Lane, passing St. Edmunds Church on your right. Follow the road to its end, with houses on your left and sports fields on your right. Cross the disused railway line and follow the well-defined path across the field, keeping to the lefthand one after a short distance. Ahead can be seen Cusworth Hall. Bear left past the cottage and left in between the lakes, and keep on the path with the lakes on your immediate right. Paths from here lead into the grounds of Cusworth Hall.

Keep on the path/track along the edge of the field, and after 1/4 mile follow the path to your left into a small wood and on across a field to the tunnel beneath the Al. Pass through this and continue ahead on the defined path. A little over 1/4 mile later, and almost at a large barn, turn left onto another path and reach the Sprotbrough Road by a path sign. Turn right, and a few yards later just before the Ivanhoe Inn turn left down Melton Gardens, as footpath-sign-posted—"Thorpe Lane". Partway down the drive turn right through the small metal gate and cross the cricket field to a stone stile and path sign. Turn left to the Church and right along Main Street. Just after entering Cadeby Road, turn left as path signed, with the Middle School on your right. Descend the drive, and at the house entrance bear right on the path and follow it round before descending eventually to steps, path sign and the Boat Inn opposite. Turn left to Sprotbrough Bridge where you began.

CUSWORTH HALL—built in 1740 by George Platt for William Wrightson and later altered by James Paine. The chapel has ornate plasterwork by Joseph Rose and the grounds were landscaped in the 1760's. The hall is now a museum of South Yorkshire life.

RIVER DON AND SPROTBROUGH LOCK.

START OF THE ELSECAR BRANCH
OF THE DEARNE & DOVE CANAL.

THE DEARNE & DOVE CANAL

Much of the history of this canal is intertwined with the Barnsley Canal. Like that one it was authorised in 1793 and open in 1804, Running from the River Don at Swinton through locks it proceeded northwards to the Barnsley Canal at Junction Lock. Two side branches were made to take in the major coal mines at Elsecar and Worsborough. The Worsborough branch was closed in 1906 due to continual subsidence and the remainder of the canal was abandoned in 1961 with serious subsidence.

Shortly after opening 720 tons of coal was carried down the canal from Elsecar; soon rising to 70,000 tons a year. In 1823 a waggon of coal at the pit head coast 12 shillings 6 pence (62p) . With transport costs to Sheffield it cost 24 shlinngs and 3 pence (£1.21p). In 1810 2,334 boats used the canal carrying 73,000 tons of coal - made up of 22,000 tons from the Barnsley Canal; 20,000 tons from Worsbough and 27,000 from Elsecar. 1805 boats advertised that they left Doncaster on Saturday evening and arrived at Barnsley on Tuesday. For a while it was a very prosperous canal with a dividend in 1804 of £8,347.50. In 1810 - £11,970 was paid out and in 1826 - £15,000.

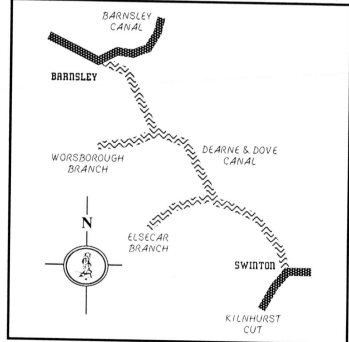

**RESTORATION PLAQUE NEAR
JUNCTION LOCK, BARNSLEY.**

DEARNE & DOVE CANAL Nr. WOMBWELL.

SWINTON LOCKS TO ELSECAR BRANCH - 5 MILES

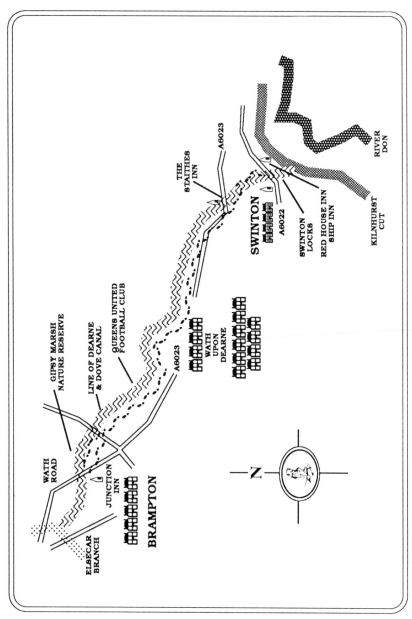

SWINTON LOCKS TO ELSECAR BRANCH - 5 miles - One Way.

- allow 2 hours.

Swinton Locks at A6022 - Dove & Dearne Canal Towpath - Bow Broom - A6023 - Wath Upon Dearne - Hollowgate - Old Moor Bridge - Gypsy Marsh Nature Reserve - The Junction Inn, Wath Road (A6023).

O.S. 1:25,000 Pathfinder Series Sheet No. SK 49/59 - Rotherham. - Sheet No. SE40/50 - Doncaster and Dearne.

No official one. Roadside parking at the locks on Broomville Street. Grid Ref. SK 463992.

Ship Inn, The Towpath, and Red House Inn at Swinton. The Staithes Inn near Wath. The Hollies, Wath. The Junction Inn, Brampton.

ABOUT THE WALK - The aim is simply to trace the line of the Dove and Dearne Canal from its junction with the Kilnhurst Cut on the Don Navigation to the Elsecar branch. It is a one-way walk but does make an enjoyable 10 mile return walk with The Junction Inn as the halfway point. The locks at Swinton are a delightful but sad sight. You follow the water filled canal for a short distance before it is filled in and almost lost. For the rest of the walk you follow the canal's basic line sometimes seeing overgrown sections, other times none at all, and pass a few canal bridges. It is very much a historical walk and although close to habitation still retains a peaceful passage through industry, mining and modern life.

WALKING INSTRUCTIONS - From the A6022 road where it crosses the canal beside the Ship Inn and Towpath Inn, gain the righthand side (Ship Inn side) of the canal and the towpath. Follow the towpath under the road bridge and continue beside the canal on your left for 1/4 mile to a railway bridge. Pass under, noticing the metal bars still bearing the rope grooves from the horse drawn boats.

Keep to the righthand of the field following a distinctive path. Where it forks keep to the right and walk beside the railway line on your right. On your left is the canal. Follow the railway line for just over 1/4 mile before bearing left following another on your right with the overgrown canal on your left. A short distance later bear right along a defined path to reach a minor road with the South Yorks NCB offices on your left and training area just ahead.

Cross the road and continue on a path past the training complex and storage area on your right. Basically keep straight ahead and just over 1/4 mile gain the A6023 road (Doncaster road) with The Staithes Inn on your right. Cross the road to your left and gain a minor road running parallel. Walk along this - the canal line - passing Charlie Brown's motor centre. At the end of the road where it turns to the A6023 road turn right onto a path passing Graham Fennell's plant on your right. After a few yards on your left you can see a canal road bridge. The canal line is now discernable being fenced. Continue on the path by the fence and passing houses on your left. After 1/2 mile reach a road with playing fields beyond. Turn left and right and follow the path along Biscay Way. On your left is The Hollies Inn.

Continue on this road to Wath Swimming Pool. Here turn right down the road for a 100 yards to a path sign. Turn left along the path with Kwik Save on your left. The canal here is lost. The path reaches another road - Whitworth Way. Cross this as path signed and follow the path to a twin tunnel. Take the righthand one and walk along the low tunnel on a concrete path. Just beyond the other side turn right and ascend the curing path onto the canal line. The path (fenced) soon swings left and in 1/4 mile gains a canal bridge. Continue ahead on the path and in a further 1/2 mile pass the Queens United Football Club on your right. Just after you follow a track round to your right with the houses of Hollowgate on your left. Where the track descends turn left and follow a path with the intermittent canal remains on your left. Keep on this for over 1/2 mile to the Brampton/Broomhill road with the Dearne Valley Technical Park just ahead to your right.

The canal line is now lost again but by crossing the road to your left and cross the field and football field you can follow its line to the A6023 road and The Junction Inn on your right. Alternatively, you can turn right along the minor road and in 1/4 mile turn left on a footpath across the Gypsy Marsh Nature Reserve. At first it is a concrete path then an ordinary path. Cross the old railway line beyond and bear right past another marshy area before gaining the Wath Road - A6023 road. The Junction Inn is to your left. To reach the Elsecar branch turn right and at the road junction a little later turn left and in 100 yards on your right is the water filled Elsecar branch.

ELSECAR GREENWAY ROUTE SIGN.

ELSECAR BRANCH OF DEARNE & DOVE
- COAL MINE LOADING BASIN, NEAR ELSECAR.

ELSECAR AND WORSBROUGH BRANCHES - 13 MILES

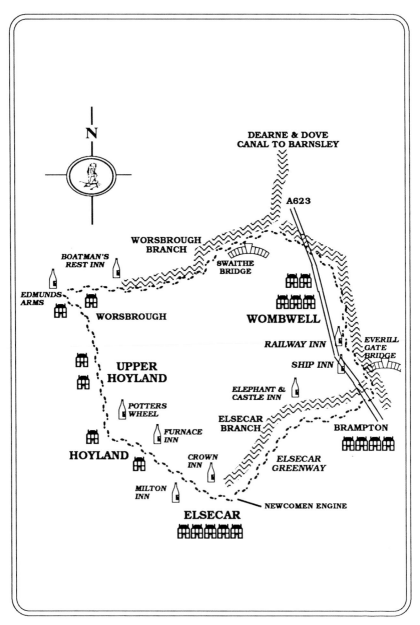

N

DEARNE & DOVE
CANAL TO BARNSLEY

A623

WORSBROUGH
BRANCH

BOATMAN'S
REST INN

SWAITHE
BRIDGE

EDMUNDS
ARMS

WORSBROUGH

WOMBWELL

RAILWAY INN

EVERILL
GATE
BRIDGE

UPPER
HOYLAND

SHIP INN

ELEPHANT &
CASTLE INN

POTTERS
WHEEL

ELSECAR
BRANCH

BRAMPTON

FURNACE
INN

HOYLAND

ELSECAR
GREENWAY

CROWN
INN

MILTON
INN

NEWCOMEN ENGINE

ELSECAR

DOVE & DEARNE CANAL -
ELSECAR AND WORSBROUGH BRANCHES - 13 miles
- allow 5 hours.

Brampton - Elsecar Branch - Tingle Bridge - Elsecar - Milton - Hoyland - Upper Hoyland - High Royd Farm - Short Wood Dike - Worsbrough - Worsbrough Dale - Lewden Hills - Worsbrough Branch - Swaithe - Dove & Dearne Canal - Wombwell - Brampton.

- O.S. 1:25,000 Pathfinder Series Sheet No. SE 40/50 - Doncaster and Dearne.
- Sheet No. SE 20/30 - Barnsley and Penistone.

No official one. Free car park just off the route at Elsecar. Roadside parking at Brampton on the B6089 Rotherham road.

Elephant & Castle, Tingle Bridge. Milton Inn and Crown Inn, Elsecar. Furnace Inn, Milton. Potters Wheel, Hoyland. Edmunds Arms, Worsbrough. Boatman's Rest, Worsbrough Dale. The Railway Inn, Wombwell.

ABOUT THE WALK - By far the longest in the book! My aim has simply been to join the Elsecar and Worsbrough branches of the Dove & Dearne Canal together. As a result it is a long walk but a very enjoyable and interesting one tracing and discovering sections of the abandoned canal. The Elsecar branch is now part of the Elsecar Greenway and the towpath has been upgraded for use. There are locks, a magnificent canal basin beside an old coal mine and a canal side inn - the Elephant & Castle to visit. The crossing to Worsborough Dale is very enjoyable with Worsbrough village worth more than a casual glance. You can extend the walk here by a mile to visit Worsbrough Mill. The Worsborough branch comes as a delightful surprise with the Boatman's Rest. At first the canal line is patchy but gets better lower down. To return to Brampton and the Elsecar branch you follow the line of the main canal. Again in places it is water filled and others filled in, but always an intriguing walk.

WALKING INSTRUCTIONS - Starting from the B6089 Rotherham road in Brampton, just off the A6023 Wath Road, gain access onto the towpath via a metal gate. The path keeps the canal on your right and at this point is well preserved and water filled. After 1/2 mile pass under a footbridge over the canal; the bridge walls have rope grooves. In a further 1/4 mile you cross a small footbridge over a canal spillway and just after pass the remains of a lock. A few yards later reach minor road from Hemingfield. The wooden post here has the plaque - Elsecar Greenway. Cross the road and continue on the well defined towpath and in less than 1/2 mile gain another road from Hemingfield at Tingle Bridge. On the otherside to your right is the Elephant and Castle Inn.

Continue beside the canal passing a series of locks and 1/4 mile from the road on your left are some excellent canal loading docks beside an old coal mine. The stonework of the wharfs is particularly excellent. Continue on the towpath and in 1/2 mile gain the road from Elsecar. Continue passing more lock remains for just over 1/4 mile to the canal's end. On your right is Dawsons and just after gain the National Coal Board road with impressive buildings just to your right. Here you begin the cross over to the Worsborough branch. Turn right to the main road in Elsecar, the B6097. Cross to your right and walk up the grass park aiming for the top lefthand corner where there is a walled path. The path to here is undefined across the open field with houses on your left. On your right is Old Row. At the top of the walled path cross the road from Hoyland. To your right is the Crown Inn and to your left the Milton Inn. Continue ahead on an unadopted road which soon becomes a path as you ascend gently and cross a railway line. Continue ahead on the wide path with football fields to your right. In 1/4 mile gain the road in Milton with two ponds ahead and the Furnace Inn on your right.

Cross the road and follow the tarmaced path above the ponds with the houses on your left. Where it forks keep to the right one and continue ascending curving to your right. At first it is open fields then you bear left with houses on your immediate right. Keep on this path to the Potter's Wheel Inn and Shaftsbury Drive. Cross the road and walk past the inn on its right to another tarmaced path. Turn right and follow this and soon ascend past houses. At the top the path forks keep to the lefthand one passing allotments on your right and houses on your left. In a short distance you reach a road which you follow to its end to the main Hoyland road. On your left is West Street Post Office and just to your right is the cenotaph.

Go straight across and follow Kirk Balk road passing the school on your left and cemetery higher up. At the crossroads beyond continue ahead on the Upper Hoyland Road. In 1/2 mile follow the zig-zag road through the houses of Upper Hoyland. Beyond ignore the turning to your left and not long after where the road turns left, leave it here and follow the farm road to High Royd Farm. Almost immediately it turns right. You keep ahead on a track with the farm buildings on your right. You soon reach an old railway line and the track turns left over it before turning right the other side. Continue on the defined path which is gated and stiled and in 1/4 mile reach a stile on the edge of Short Wood. Follow the path down to your right and cross the Short Wood Dike and continue on the path ascending close to the field edge to a cottage. Just beyond it turn left along a track and in 1/2 mile gain Worsbrough village close to St. Mary's church. Turn right along the road passing the Edmunds Arms on your left. Keep on the main road passing Worsbrough Hall also on your left. If you want to extend the walk you can just past the inn turn left and follow the path signs to Worsbrough Mill.

Keep on the road a little further to where it turns left. Here continue ahead on the tarmaced track and pass Park Cottages on your left. Just after turn left, as footpath signed. The path almost immediately turns right and you walk along a sunken hedged path and in 1/4 mile reach a crossroads of paths. Keep straight ahead on the track for the next 1/2 mile. On your left is the boundary of Worsbrough Country Park. At the end of the track turn left and cross the bridge and gain the Worsbrough branch with the Boatman's Rest Inn just ahead. Continue past the inn and turn right along Oak Close. At the end bear left past the houses to a stile before a stone house. Walk past this to another stile and follow the defined path across the fields to Lewden Farm 1/4 mile. The actual canal line is to your right.

Walk past the lefthand side of the farm to the road and path sign Goose Hulls. Turn left up the road a few yards before turning right up a track, as footpath signed over Lewden Hills. The path bears right and keeps above a wood before descending to its edge. Just after don't descend to the river Dove but bear left passing under the railway archway. Keep to the righthand edge of the field with the hedge on your right to the site of Swaithe Bridge. Here the canal location is more discerable with the fencing. Follow the track with the fencing on your left and in 1/2 mile gain a stile. After this the canal is no longer filled in and quite recognisable. Just afterwards the canal turns sharp left, here you turn right and descend on a well defined path to a stile. Continue to your right once more following the line of (main) canal to another stile and the remains of a railway bridge. Cross another stile and keep to the righthand edge of the field to Aldham Mill - horse stables. Do not cross the river but keep to the right of the stables to a stile and cross the field to another by a path sign at the entrance to the mill.

Cross the A633 Wath road and walk along the lefthand side of the canal and soon pass under a former railway bridge with good examples of rope grooves. Continue following the line of the canal although industry has covered part of it. In more than 1/4 mile gain the National Coal Board road. To your right is the White Rose Inn. Cross the road to a stile and continue now in sparse woodland following the line of the canal. In 1/4 mile cross the Wombwell bypass road and continue on the canal line. In a further 1/4 mile cross a minor road by B & H Motors of Wombwell with the Wombwell Karting Track well to your left. The canal is now filled in but a tarmaced path basically traces its line with the bypass on your left and in 1/4 mile reach a roundabout with the The Railway Inn on your left and the Peace Gardens on your right.

Basically continue ahead now following a well defined path with unfilled canal on your right. In 1/4 mile pass a bridge with rope grooves and in another 1/2 mile reach the Everill Gate Lane. Cross this and continue by the canal which is quite excellent here and in 1/4 mile reach the Wath Road. Turn right then left onto the B6089 Rotherham road and retrace your steps back to your starting out point At Brampton.

ELSECAR BRANCH Nr. BRAMPTON.

**ELEPHANT & CASTLE INN, TINGLE BRIDGE
- ELSECAR BRANCH.**

**BOATMAN'S REST
- WORSBROUGH
BRANCH.**

THE BARNSLEY CANAL

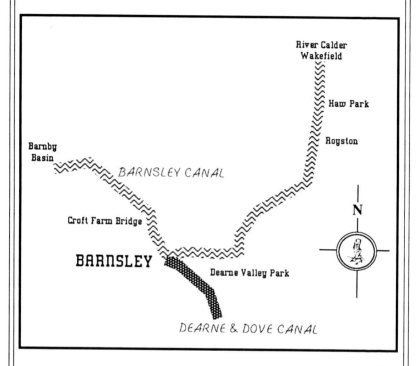

The coal mine proprietors were the prime movers behind this canal which was authorised in 1793 and opened in 1804. The builder was William Jessop and the principal workforce was managed by the Pinkerton family. The canal ran from the River Calder at Wakefield to Barnsley and its junction with the Dearne & Dove Canal. Here the canal turned north-westerly to take in the Silkstone coalfields at Barnaby Basin. In 1819 the canal was carrying over 95,000 tons of coal, 23,000 tons of limestone, 21 quaters of corn, 2,000 tons of lime, 1,000 tons of iron, 800 tons of timber, 11,000 tons of miscelleaneous material and considerable mining equipment was carried to the expanding coalfields. Worsbough Coal was taken via the Dearne & Dove into the Barnsley Canal and taken to the River Calder at Wakefield. Like all canals it suffered from the competition of railways and as it was primarily a coal orientated canal and not being part of a major link system it fell into steady decline. By the 1950's it was abandoned.

**EARLY PART OF SILKSTONE BRANCH
Nr. SMITHY BRIDGE.**

BARNSLEY CANAL, Nr. WALTON (WAKEFIELD).

CENTRAL BARNSLEY
- 2 MILES

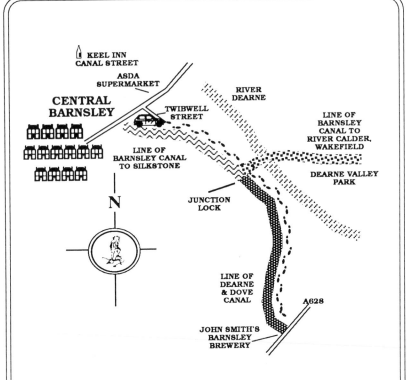

KEEL INN
CANAL STREET

ASDA
SUPERMARKET

RIVER
DEARNE

CENTRAL
BARNSLEY

TWIBWELL
STREET

LINE OF
BARNSLEY
CANAL TO
RIVER CALDER,
WAKEFIELD

LINE OF
BARNSLEY CANAL
TO SILKSTONE

DEARNE VALLEY
PARK

N

JUNCTION
LOCK

LINE OF
DEARNE
& DOVE
CANAL

A628

JOHN SMITH'S
BARNSLEY
BREWERY

SOUTH YORKSHIRE EMBLEM FOOTPATH SIGN.

BARNSLEY CANAL -
CENTRAL BARNSLEY
- 2 miles - allow 1 hour.

Twibwell Street Car Park - Barnsley Canal - Junction Lock - John Smiths (Barnsley Brewery) - A628 - return same way.

- O.S. - 1:25,000 Pathfinder Series Sheet No. SE 20/30 - Barnsley & Penistone.

- Just off Twibwell Street - Grid Ref. SE 353070.

- None on the walk. Nearest and on the canal - The Keel Inn, Canal Street.

ABOUT THE WALK - A short walk to explore the junction of the Barnsley and Dearne & Dove Canals. The area has been restored with the impressive Junction Lock to see, a section of waterfilled canal, and a footbridge where the Barnsley Aqueduct ran across the River Dearne. Much of the walk is the Dearne Valley Park and neatly joins other canal walks to extend the walk if time permits. You can follow the line of the canal (Dearne & Dove) from Junction Lock to the A628 road beside John Smiths - the former Barnsley Brewery. The canal beyond is lost and cannot really be picked up again until near the start of the A633 Wath Upon Dearne road at Stairfoot; here is the Keel Inn with an inn sign of a canal boat.

CANAL STREET AND KEEL INN.

WALKING INSTRUCTIONS - From the car you can turn right and walk along the line e of the canal to the main road. Cross this to reach Canal Skeet and the Keel Inn. On the main route turn left and soon reach the canal on your right and walk along the tarmaced path. In 1/4 mile reach the junction where the Barnsley Canal turns left to cross the River Dearne and begin its journey to the Wakefield and the River Calder. There is a footbridge over the aqueduct supports, with the Dearne Valley beyond. At the junction are the remains of the lockeeper's cottage and two stone pillars, on either side of the canal, upon which the horse's rope was looped to pull the boat around the sharp corner. Having explored the "aqueduct" continue beside the canal - now the Dearne & Dove - and reach the well preserved junction lock . You can continue following the line of the canal from here to the A628 road. Return the same way back to the car park at Twibwell Street.

JUNCTION OF BARNSLEY CANAL AND DEARNE & DOVE CANAL - NOTICE THE ROPE PULLEY PILLARS ON EITHER SIDE OF THE CANAL.

JUNCTION LOCK - DEARNE & DOVE CANAL.

KEEL INN - CANAL STREET, BARNSLEY.

45

DEARNE VALLEY PARK
- 4 MILES

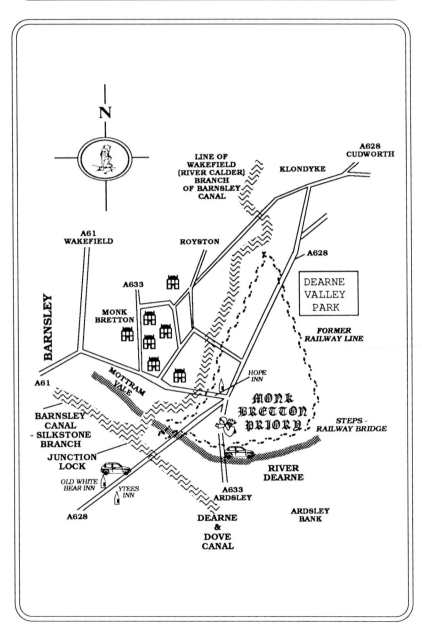

N

LINE OF
WAKEFIELD
(RIVER CALDER)
BRANCH
OF BARNSLEY
CANAL

KLONDYKE

A628
CUDWORTH

A61
WAKEFIELD

ROYSTON

A628

A633

DEARNE
VALLEY
PARK

MONK
BRETTON

BARNSLEY

FORMER
RAILWAY LINE

HOPE
INN

A61

MOTTRAM
VALE

MONK
BRETTON
PRIORY

STEPS -
RAILWAY BRIDGE

BARNSLEY
CANAL
- SILKSTONE
BRANCH

JUNCTION
LOCK

OLD WHITE
BEAR INN

YTEES
INN

A633
ARDSLEY

RIVER
DEARNE

ARDSLEY
BANK

A628

DEARNE
&
DOVE
CANAL

BARNSLEY CANAL
DEARNE VALLEY PARK
4 miles
—allow 2 hours

  —*Monk Bretton Priory—Lundwood—Klondyke—Lundwood Bridge— Hoyle Mill—River Dearne—Monk Bretton Priory.*

  —*O.S.l:50,000—Sheet No 111—Sheffield & Doncaster area.*
—*O.S.1;25,000—Sheet No SE 20/30—Barnsley and Penistone.*
—*Dearne Valley Park leaflet.*

—*Monk Bretton Priory, off Abbey Lane at Cundy Cross.*

- *Kirsty's Inn, Klondyke; Hope Inn, Cundy Cross; and Old White Bear Inn and Ytees Inn just off the route.*

ABOUT THE WALK—starting from Monk Bretton Priory, which can be explored before or after the walk, you encircle the Dearne Valley Park following old railway lines, and over mining spoil heaps. The park is an imaginative scheme reclaiming an industrial area and converting it into a leisure complex. It is an exciting project and the following walk explores a major part of it, following the line of the old Barnsley Canal, old railways and mining areas. Much of the path is tarmaced and makes an ideal walk for all the family in an area which comes as a surprise amidst housing and an industrial complex. Although I have started the walk from Monk Bretton Priory, you can start from Barnsley itself and explore a restored section of the Barnsley Canal, adding an extra mile to the whole route - see Central Barnsley walk.

WALKING INSTRUCTIONS—From Monk Bretton Priory car park turn right down the path into the park and main walkway. Turn left along it heading towards the railway bridge. Far to your right is the River Dearne which you near at the bridge. Ascend the steps to the top of the bridge and turn left along the disused railway line. After 1/4 mile you cross a minor road and continue along the "line" on a tarmaced path. 1/4 mile still on the tarred path pass under the road and 1/4 mile later near the Klondyke road and canal bridge. A little to your left beside the road is Kirsty's Inn. Keep within the park and turn left on the path with a former mine spoil heap on your left. The pathline is now following the line of the Barnsley canal.

After more than 1/2 mile you near a road at Lundwood and swing left to a stile. Cross the road and continue ahead on the path, which after 1/4 mile reaches the Hope Inn and road at Cundy Cross. Cross over then descend into the Dearne Valley and bear right along the line of another railway. After 1/4 mile take the track on your left and descend to the footbridge with the small lake on your right. Cross the River Dearne and left to a car park with the Ytees Inn just beyond. Keep on the path out of the car park, with the road—A628 on your right. Reach the road via the stile before the road bridge. Turn left over the bridge and right at the stile to continue on the tarmaced path through the valley. A little over 1/4 mile later reach the road at Cundy Cross and turn left then right back into Monk Bretton car park.

MONK BRETTON—founded for monks of the Cluniac Order in 1153 by Adam Fitzswein. In 1281 the monks were of the Benedictine order. In 1538 the priory was closed and many of the buildings were stripped. The north aisle was rebuilt at Wentworth church and other parts were converted to a private residence. In 1932 it came under the care of the then Ministry of Works, and is today well worth exploring to see the ruins, 15th century gatehouse, the Prior's chamber and 14th century guesthouse.

BARNSLEY CANAL - CROFT FARM BRIDGE.

BARNSLEY CANAL Nr. CROFT FARM BRIDGE.

SILKSTONE BRANCH
2,5,& 7 MILES

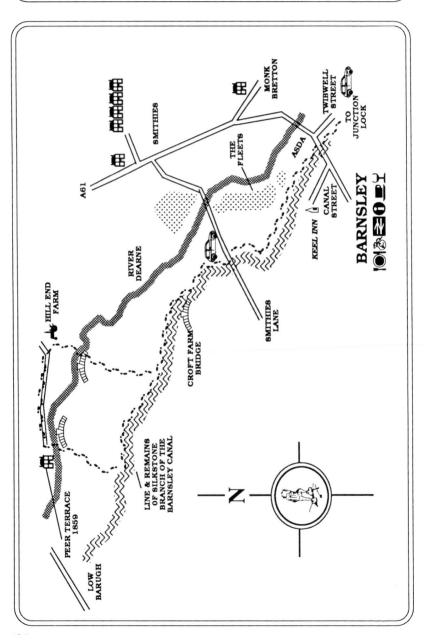

BARNSLEY CANAL -
SILKSTONE BRANCH
5 miles, 2 miles & 7 miles.
- allow 2, 1 and 3 hours.

 - *Smithies Lane Car Park - Barnsley Canal - River Dearne - Lower Carr Green - Hill End Farm - River Dearne - Barnsley Canal - Smithies Lane Car Park.*

EXTENSION - Smithies Lane Car Park - line of Barnsley Canal - Honeywell - Central Barnsley - return same way.

 O.S. - 1:25,000 Pathfinder Series Sheet No. SE 20/30 - Barnsley & Penistone.

 Smithies Lane, beside the canal at Grid Ref. SE347079.

- Keel Inn, Canal Street, Central Barnsley.

ABOUT THE WALK - Westwards from the carpark, the canal is magnificent, full of surprises and full of features - quaint bridges, mooring jetties and impressive towpath. Upon reaching the end of the canal instead of simply retracing your steps you walk across the fields and cross the River Dearne to near Mapplewell. You cross another footbridge over the River Dearne before rejoining the canal and following back to the car park. The walk can be extended by a couple of miles towards central Barnsley and the Keel Inn. Enroute you pass a solitary stone pulley block; a feature of the Barnsley Canal. You continue onto Junction Lock or even start from the Twibwell Street car park to make an even longer walk.

WALKING INSTRUCTIONS - From the car park beside Smithies Lane, walk away from the road beside the reed filled canal on a good path. For the next couple of miles you keep the canal on your right to its end. En route pass the impressive bridge close to Croft Farm. A little further and you cross a large metal stile. 1/2 mile later another footbridge but this one is level. 1/2 mile later and where the canal ends or rather is filled in where the electric transmission line

51

crosses the canal, continue ahead on a cinder path to the field fence. Bear right still on the path and keep the fence on your left, with a dike beyond, and reach a footbridge. Cross this and continue on a fenced path to another footbridge, this time over the River Dearne. Keep to the lefthand edge of the field and reach the road infront of Peer Terrace built in 1859, by a path sign.

Turn right and walk along the lane for 1/2 mile and turn right along Hill End Road. Where it turns sharp left and ascends opposite Hill End Farm, keep straight ahead to a stile and another just after. Beyond turn right on a well defined path between the bushes and in 1/4 mile reach a footbridge over the River Dearne. Cross and angle slightly left across the field, walking beside a fence on your left in the final stages and regain the canal. Turn left and soon pass the flat footbridge across it before gaining the metal stile. Continue beside the canal and retrace your steps back to Smithies Lane.

You can extend this walk by crossing Smithies Lane and following the signposted path along the line of the canal. It is a broad swath with a housing estate on your right. On your left is The Fleets a popular fishing area. The path comes out on the right of the Asda superstore with the Keel Inn on your right. If you cross the main roads from Canal Street you can continue along the green swath to the Twibwell Street car park and onto the Junction Lock and "aqueduct" over the River Dearne and the Dearne Valley Park.

BARNSLEY CANAL - CROFT FARM BRIDGE.

52

BARNSLEY CANAL AT HAW PARK.

BARNSLEY CANAL - BRIDGE Nr. WALTON
- NOTICE ROPE GROOVES ON RIGHT.

ROYSTON - 3 MILES

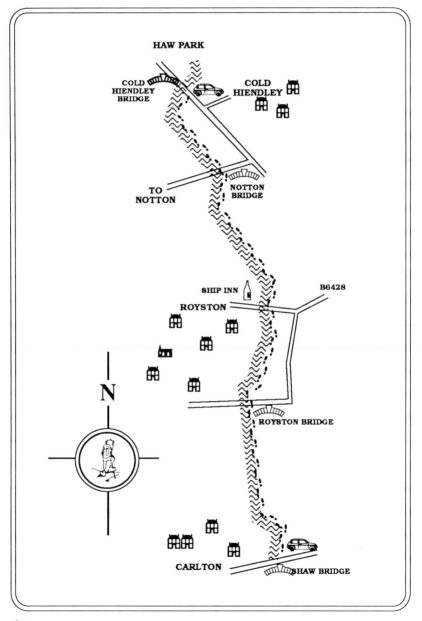

BARNSLEY CANAL -
ROYSTON - 3 miles
- one way. - allow 1 hour.

- *Being a one-way walk you can start the walk from either end or in the middle! Cold Hiendley - Royston - Carlton (Shaw Lane).* ·

- *O.S - 1:50,000 Landranger Series Sheet No. 111 - Sheffield & Doncaster area.*
  - O.S. 1:25,000 Pathfinder Series Sheet No. 703 (SE21/31)
  - Wakefield (south) and area.

- *No official one but roadside parking at the Cold Hiendley end at Grid Ref. SE 366143. Also at Shaw Lane Grid Ref. SE 373101.*

- *Ship Inn, Royston, on the B6428 - Royston/Ryhill road.*

ABOUT THE WALK - The northern half of the canal is water filled and near Notton the canal passes through a spectacular gorge. Around Royston it is largely full of weeds. The canal makes enjoyable walking tracing the line of the visible canal from near Cold Hiendley in the north to Shaw Lane near Carlton in the south. Half the walk is in West Yorkshire and the rest in South Yorkshire - the canal forming the county boundary just north of the B6428 road.

WALKING INSTRUCTIONS - Starting from the Cold Hiendley end the towpath keeps to the lefthand side (the eastern side) of the canal all the way to Shaw Lane, Carlton.

HAW PARK - 4 MILES

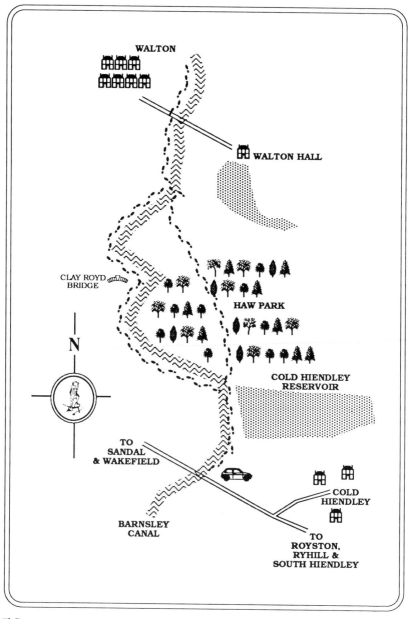

WALTON

WALTON HALL

CLAY ROYD
BRIDGE

HAW PARK

N

COLD HIENDLEY
RESERVOIR

TO
SANDAL
& WAKEFIELD

COLD
HIENDLEY

BARNSLEY
CANAL

TO
ROYSTON,
RYHILL &
SOUTH HIENDLEY

- Cold Hiendley Reservoir - Haw Park - Barnsley Canal - Overtown Bridge - Walton Hall Bridge - Walton Lock - Barnsley Canal - Cold Hiendley Reservoir.

 - O.S. 1:50,000 Landranger Series Sheet No.111 - Sheffield & Doncaster area.
- O.S. 1:25,000 Pathfinder Series Sheet No. 703 (SE@!/31) - Wakefield (South) & area.

- No official one but roadside parking at start of the walk at Grid Ref. SE 366143. Further parking along the track you walk beside Cold Hiendley Reservoir at Grid Ref. SE 367146.

- None on the walk. The nearest are at Notton and Wintersett.

ABOUT THE WALK - Quite simply a magnificent walk - in fact one of the best canal walks I have done! First you walk past Cold Hiendley Reservoir before walking through Haw Park forest, which in autumn is particularly attractive. Leaving the wood behind you gain the abandoned Barnsley Canal and walk beside it to the remains of Walton Lock. Here you turn round and walk back along the canal to Cold Hiendley Reservoir. The scenery is most attractive and the canal beautifully engineered through a cutting and around the forest. En route are abandoned bridges and a feature I have never seen before in over 1,000 miles of canal walking - a guiding pulley for the horse rope around sharp corners of the canal. This walk although just inside West Yorkshire is a walk of great historical importance and an absorbing exploration of canals.

WALKING INSTRUCTIONS - Starting from the road just before the canal, turn right onto the track with the canal on your left, as you walk to Cold Hiendley Reservoir. There is car parking space here. Continue along the lefthand edge of the reservoir and cross a footbridge to reach Haw Park forest. There are three paths here; take the middle one; the one on your left is the one you will return on. Walk through the wood mostly on a track and keep straight ahead at all junctions in little over ™ mile you begin to descend and soon reach a stile close to a path sign - Cold Hiendley. Here you leave the forest behind and continue on a well defined path to the canal, which comes in from your left. Continue to a bridge over the canal and cross it. Just after turn right, as footpath signed and follow a path through the trees and down to the canal towpath. Don't turn right along the towpath; keep ahead instead on the towpath to Walton Hall bridge which has rope grooves. Cross the road and continue on the path to see the ruins of Walton Lock.

Here you turn round and retrace your steps back to Walton Hall bridge and to the towpath junction. Here you keep ahead on the towpath passing under the bridge you crossed earlier. You keep beside the canal on your left for the next mile as it passes through a cutting, and around Haw Park. En route passing bridges and two stone pulley posts. Near the end you walk along a filled in section before regaining the water filled canal. Shortly after pass under a bridge and regain your starting out path at the footbridge. Cross this and retrace your steps back to the road.

**ROPE PULLEY PILLAR
- BARNSLEY CANAL IN HAW PARK.**

BARNSLEY CANAL IN HAW PARK.

ARKSEY & BENTLEY COMMON - 5 MILES

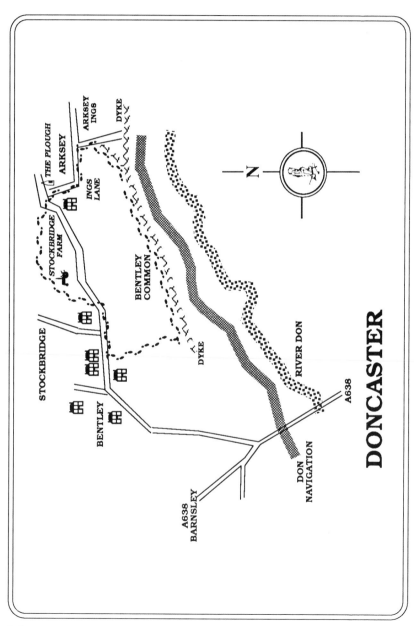

60

ARKSEY & BENTLEY COMMON - 5 miles

- allow 2 hours.

- Arksey - Stockbridge - Bentley - Bentley Common - Ings Lane - Arksey.

- O.S. 1:25,000 Pathfinder Series Sheet No. SE 40/50 - Doncaster and Dearne.

- No official car park but roadside parking beside Arksey church at Grid Ref. SE579069.

- The Plough Inn, Arksey.

ABOUT THE WALK- Not a canal walk! But a walk in a very attractive area close to the canal. I wanted to include a walk to the north of Doncaster along the canal but it proved impracticable so I opted for this one. It does include a major dike walk which is a major feature of walking in the eastern side of the county, as my walks have shown. Arksey is an attractive village which still retains several old buildings despite considerable modem buildings. You will pass the church, Almshouses dated 1660, and see Arksey Hall and the earthworks of a Round About Moat. You cross fields and lanes to Bentley and once past the ever expanding complex of Doncaster Cables reach a track and open countryside. For the remainder of the walk you have quiet lanes and impressive dike across Bentley Common to follow. You will see a variety of waterfowl and numerous drains and stretches of water.

WALKING INSTRUCTIONS - Starting from the church at Arksey, walk along High Street past the 1660 Almshouses and school, and follow the road round to your right, passing The Plough Inn on your right. At the end of the street turn left; to your right is Arksey Hall. In a short distance the road turns right; here you keep ahead on a footpath signed track. As you approach the railway line on your left is the earthworks of the Round About Moat. Cross the railway line and a few yards later turn left on the path which parallells the railway line. After 150 yards meet a path junction and turn right on the tarmaced path, In a few yards turn left onto a track and follow this for.just over 1/4 mile to Stockbridge Lane. Follow this round to your left and in another 1/4 mile gain the main Bentley/Arksey Road close to a footpath sign.

Turn right and follow the road into Bentley and.just before the first road junction on your right and the Bentley Pentecostal Church turn left on the road into Millfields Industrial Estate. Follow the road round to your right and infront of Derek Lewis excavating depot turn right onto a fenced tarmaced path. Follow this round to the end of a small road and keep left to follow the path with the houses on your right to Millgate Lane. Before it you bear left along the path beside the perimeter fence of Doncaster Cables. Cross a small bridge and reach Millgate Lane. The original mill was near the bridge. Turn left along the lane and keep straight ahead at the junction just ahead and reach the railway line. Cross this via the small gates and in a short distance reach the top of the dike. Here turn left over the railway line fence and walk along the top of the dike for 1 1/2 miles.

The dike is high and commands goods views over Bentley Common and Bentley Ings. After about 1/2 an hour of walking you will reach a fork in the dike with a smaller wood covered one on your left. Here turn left and soon reach a stile. The path through the avenue of trees along the dike is impressive. Soon reach another stile and in 1/4 mile emerge onto the track of Ings Lane. Turn left along the track and in 1/4 mile turn left at the track junction as you head for Arksey with the church a prominent feature. After 1/2 mile enter Arksey and keep to the righthand road to gain the main road through Arksey. Turn left and in a few yards on your right is the church and road where you began.

DYKE Nr. ARKSEY.

DYKE ACROSS BENTLEY COMMON.

ARKSEY CHURCH.

THE NEW JUNCTION CANAL

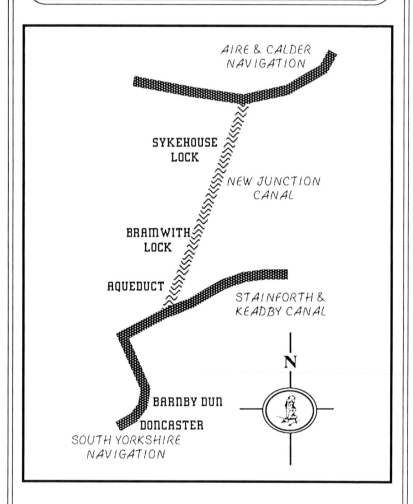

AIRE & CALDER
NAVIGATION

SYKEHOUSE
LOCK

NEW JUNCTION
CANAL

BRAMWITH
LOCK

AQUEDUCT

STAINFORTH &
KEADBY CANAL

N

BARNBY DUN

DONCASTER

SOUTH YORKSHIRE
NAVIGATION

The Sheffield and South Yorkshire Navigation Company and the Aire and Calder Navigation built the 5 1/2 mile (8.9 km) canal which opened on January 2nd 1905, connecting the two navigations together. This is the last canal to be built in Britain. In 1905 the tonnage carried along the canal was 835,982 tons with a toll revenue of £48,981. In 1913 this had risen to 961,774 tons with a revenue of £53,586.

CANTILEVER BRIDGE - NEW JUNCTION CANAL.

**SYKEHOUSE LOCK AND VIEW SOUTHWARDS
TO THORPE MARSH POWER STATION.**

BRAITHWAITE & BRAMWITH - 4 MILES

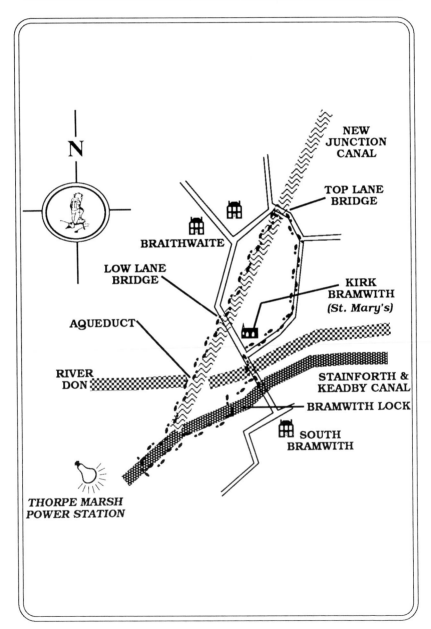

NEW JUNCTION CANAL

TOP LANE BRIDGE

BRAITHWAITE

LOW LANE BRIDGE

KIRK BRAMWITH (St. Mary's)

AQUEDUCT

RIVER DON

STAINFORTH & KEADBY CANAL

BRAMWITH LOCK

SOUTH BRAMWITH

THORPE MARSH POWER STATION

N

- Braithwaite - Low Lane Bridge - New Junction Canal - Stainforth & Keadby Canal - Bramwith Lock - South Bramwith - Kirk Bramwith - Top Lane Bridge - New Junction Canal - Low Lane Bridge,

- O.S. 1:50,000 Landranger Series Sheet No. 111 - Sheffield & Doncaster area.

- No official one - roadside parking near Low Lane Bridge and near bridge close to Barnby Dun.

- None on the walk. Nearest the Hacienda at Kirkhouse Green, a mile to the north of the walk.

ABOUT THE WALK - A short walk to explore the southern end of the New Junction Canal. There is much to see - a spectacular aqueduct over the River Don and Bramwith Lock. On the otherside of the canal is the hamlet of South Bramwith with several transport plaques on a wall near the bridge. The hamlet of Kirk Bramwith is walked though with a delightful little church. I have started the walk from Low Lane Bridge, Braithwaite, but you can start it elsewhere.

WALKING INSTRUCTIONS - From Low Lane Bridge, walk along the towpath heading southwards, keeping the canal on your lefthand side. In just over 1/2 mile cross the impressive aqueduct over the River Don with gates at either end. Do not cross the footbridge but continue beside the canal on your left passing the junction of the Stainforth & Keadby Canal in less than 1/4 mile. A further 1/4 mile brings you to the bridge over the canal, with Thorpe Marsh Power Station just ahead. Cross the bridge and turn left following the towpath with the canal on your left. In 1/2 mile pass the canal junction again and 1/4 mile later reach Bramwith Lock. Here you cross the lock gates and continue on the towpath now on the lefthand side of the canal. This is now a road which you follow to the swing bridge opposite South Bramwith.

Leave the canal here and turn left along the road and cross the bridge over the River Don and reach Kirk Bramwith church, dedicated to St. Mary. Here the road forks - to your left is a direct way back to Low Lane Bridge - but I prefer to bear right through Kirk Bramwith village and in 1/2 mile gain the New Junction Canal at Top Lane Bridge. Cross the bridge and turn left onto the towpath and follow it back to Low Lane Bridge.

**AQUEDUCT OVER RIVER DON
ON THE NEW JUNCTION CANAL.**

LOOKING NORTH TO BRAMWITH LOCK
-STAINFORTH & KEADBY CANAL.

BRAMWITH LOCK - STAINFORTH & KEADBY CANAL.

SYKEHOUSE
- 7 1/2 MILES

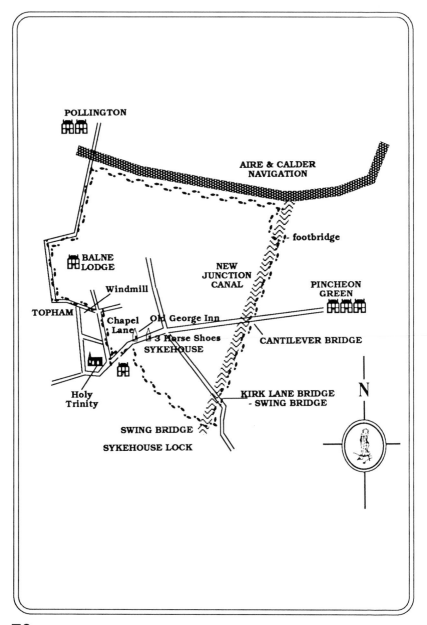

POLLINGTON

AIRE & CALDER
NAVIGATION

- footbridge

BALNE
LODGE

NEW
JUNCTION
CANAL

PINCHEON
GREEN

Windmill

TOPHAM

Chapel
Lane

Old George Inn

3 Horse Shoes
SYKEHOUSE

CANTILEVER BRIDGE

Holy
Trinity

KIRK LANE BRIDGE
- SWING BRIDGE

N

SWING BRIDGE

SYKEHOUSE LOCK

SYKEHOUSE - 7 1/2 miles
- allow 3 hours.

•▪ ▪• ▪• - *Sykehouse - Sykehouse Lock - New Junction Canal - Aire & Calder Navigation - Balne LOdge - Topham - Thorseby Hall Farm - Sykehouse.*

- O.S. 1:50,000 Landranger Series Sheet No. 111 - Sheffield & Doncaster area.

- No official car park - roadside parking near Sykehouse church.

- Old George Inn, Three Horse Shoes - Sykehouse.

ABOUT THE WALK - There are three paths in the vicinity of the church that cross the fields to Sykehouse Lock. Here you join the New Junction Canal and follow it northwards to its junction with the Aire & Calder Navigation. En route you pass swing bridges and a cantilever one. There is little traffic on the canal and you will more than likely have the towpath to your self as well. You follow the Aire & Calder Navigation for more than two miles - you are just inside Humberside at this point - to near Pollington. Here you walk inland on tracks around the fields to Topham and its former windmill. A short road walk returns you to Sykehouse church where you began,

WALKING INSTRUCTIONS - Starting on Broad Lane opposite Sykehouse church, dedicated to Holy Trinity, walk along the road away from the church - eastwards - to pass the Old George Inn on your right. Opposite the church is a footpath sign and another on the right of the inn. Continue a little further to Chapel Row and turn right at another path sign and walk along a hedged track. In a few yards reach a large open field. Keep to the lefthand side and reach a small gap on your left and its end. Keep to the field edge beyond and reach a wooden stile in a few yards. Cross the next field aiming for the far righthand corner where there is a gate. Keep to the righthand edge of the field and don't turn right to the farm but continue a little further to a small gate on your right. Turn right through this and cross the field to another gate on the lefthand side of the farm. Turn left along the track and reach the New Junction Canal; swing bridge and Sykehouse Lock.

Cross the bridge and turn left along the towpath with the canal on your left, In 1/2 mile reach Kirk Lane Bridge; a swing bridge. Continue on the righthand side of the canal and in more than 1/2 mile reach a large cantilever bridge. Continue ahead by the canal and in 3/4 mile gain a metal footbridge over the canal. Cross this and turn right, now keeping the canal on your right. Cross an aqueduct over the River Went and just beyond is the Aire & Calder Navigation. Turn left and walk along this canal, keeping it on your right for more than 2 miles. In little over a mile pass the remains of a former swing bridge. 1/2 mile later at the first bridge leave the canal and reach the road. Turn left but not sharp left, and follow the minor road towards Balne Lodge. In 1/2 mile and nearing the lodge turn right onto a track along the field field edge. In 1/4 mile where another track joins from your left, turn left and follow this track for 3/4 mile to the houses at Topham. Follow the road round to your left and in 1/4 mile at a cross roads, continue ahead and pass the former windmill on your right. At the end of the road turn right along Chapel Lane passing Thorseby Hall Farm on your left. In 1/4 mile reach Holy Trinity church where you started .

SWING BRIDGE - NEW JUNCTION CANAL.

VIEW FROM FOOTBRIDGE OVER NEW JUNCTION
CANAL - JUST AHEAD IS AQUEDUCT OVER THE
RIVER WENT AND BEYOND IS SOUTHFIELD
RESERVOIR AND THE AIRE AND CALDER
NAVIGATION.

SYKEHOUSE LOCK - LOOKING SOUTH.

STAINFORTH & KEADBY CANAL

Forms part of the Sheffield and South Yorkshire Navigation - 43 miles from Keadby on the River Trent to Sheffield. Boats up to 700 tons can now reach Rotherham, where the canal to Sheffield and its impressive flight of eleven locks at Tinsley remain much as they were originally.

In the early 18th century a canal was cut from Hadfield Chase to the River Tent - much of the basic line of the Stainforth & Keadby Canal - for carrying peat from the moorland. Part of it is still named the "boating dyke" on the Ordnance Survey maps. In 1790 between 30 and forty boats were using the drain for carrying turf. The cheaper coal brought on the canal meant the industry slowly died and ceased in the 1830's. The canal was built primarily to transport coal brought down the Dearne & Dove Canal to the River Trent and the port of Goole.

CANAL ROUTE SIGN AT THE JUNCTION OF THE NEW JUNCTION CANAL AND THE STAINFORTH & KEADBY CANAL.

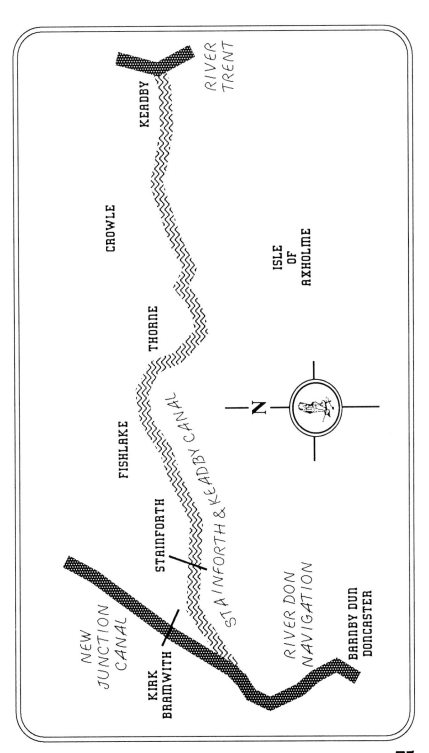

RIVER TRENT

KEADBY

CROWLE

THORNE

ISLE OF AXHOLME

FISHLAKE

N

STAINFORTH

STAINFORTH & KEADBY CANAL

NEW JUNCTION CANAL

KIRK BRAMWITH

RIVER DON NAVIGATION

BARNBY DUN
DONCASTER

THORNE - (WEST) - 8 MILES

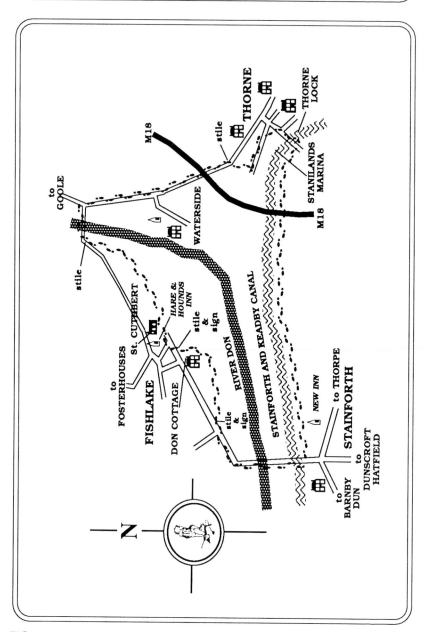

STAINFORTH & KEADBY CANAL
THORNE - (WEST) —8 miles
—allow 3 1/2 hours

⏱ ⏱ ⏱ ⏱ —*Fishlake—Stainforth—Stainforth & Keadby
Canal—Thorne Lock— Waterside—River Don—Fishlake.*

 —*O.S. 1:50,000 Landranger Sheet No. 111 - Sheffield & Doncaster area. —O.S. 1:25,000 Pathfinder Series Sheet No. SE 60/70.*

🚗 —*No official ones at Fishlake, Stainforth or Thorne Lock.*

🍺 *Hare & Hounds Inn, Fishlake; New Inn, Stainforth; and another off
the route at Waterside.*

ABOUT THE WALK—Fishlake is a particularly attractive village
steeped in history. The area was drained in the 17th Century and is
the reason you walk along dykes. First you head for Stainforth to gain
the Canal, which you follow to Thorne Lock. A very pleasant walk in
its own right is along the Canal around the southern edge of the town.
A brief road walk from the lock takes you under the M18, with the
option of exploring Waterside before walking along the dyke back to
Fishlake.

WALKING INSTRUCTIONS—Starting from the church, dedicated to St. Cuthbert in Fishlake, notice the path signs behind you
to your right—this is the way you return. Walk along Church Street
past the Hare and Hounds Inn on your right, and on past the cross
shaft, also on your right. A little further along Main Street, at the path
sign in front of Don Cottage, turn left along the path passing the
houses on your right. Shortly after a stile, gain the dyke top which
you basically follow for the next mile towards Stainforth. Where the
dyke and river almost join, bear right to a stile and path sign. Turn
left along the Fishlake road to the bridge over the River Don in
Stainforth. Once over, turn left and gain the towpath of the Stainforth
and Keadby Canal. Keeping the canal on your left, pass the New Inn
and continue beside the canal for the next 3 1/2 miles, passing under
the M18, before reaching Thorne Lock. Here the canal can be further
explored around Thorne.

Cross the canal bridge with Thorne Lock on your right, and keep left to gain a footpath past the houses to a lane and path sign—Stainforth. Turn left along the tarmaced lane, passing under the railway before reaching a sharp lefthand junction and gated farm road. Keep ahead on a track, and at the gate turn right on a path keeping the field boundary on your right. Continue around a field to a stile and A614 road. Turn left and pass under the M18, and shortly afterwards you can turn left along Waterside Road to the hamlet and inn above the marsh and nearby River Don. Return to the A614 road and turn left and follow it to the Fishlake road junction and turn left. Just after crossing the River Don turn left at the stile and gain the dyke. Keep on this for a little over two miles back to Fishlake. The church tower serves as a useful landmark, and when almost opposite it leave the dyke and descend to the path sign, stile and track into Fishlake where you began.

FISHLAKE—church dedicated to St. Cuthbert and largely of 13th—15th century workmanship. The south porch has one of the best Norman doorways in England.

THORNE LOCK - STAINFORTH & KEADBY CANAL.

BOAT GOING THROUGH THORNE LOCK
- STAINFORTH & KEADBY CANAL.

STAINFORTH & KEADBY CANAL NEAR CROWLE.

THORNE (EAST)
- 4 MILES

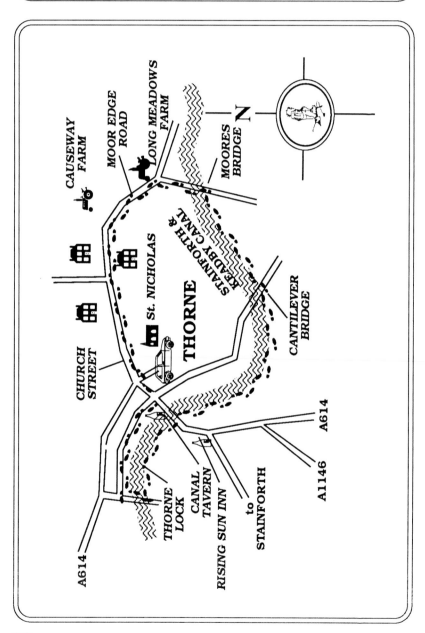

Thorne Church Car Park - Thorne Lock - Stainforth & Keadby Canal - Moores Bridge - Moores Edge Road - Thorne Church.

- O.S. 1:50,000 Landranger Series Sheet No. 111 - Sheffield & Doncaster area and Sheet No. 112 - Scunthorpe.

- Off Church Street in front of St. Nicholas church at Grid. Ref., SE 689133.

- Several in central Thorne including the Red Bear. On the canal in Thorne are the Rising Sun Inn and Canal Tavern.

ABOUT THE WALK - The canal around Thorne is particularly attractive, as this walk illustrates. First you walk through the town to Thorne Lock and follow the canal in a semi-circle around Thorne for 2 miles to Moores Bridge. Here you leave the canal and follow lane and minor roads back to Thorne church. A very pleasant walk with an attractive town to explore en route.

WALKING INSTRUCTIONS - Return to the main road - Church Balk - and turn left to the A614 road. Cross over into the shopping area and take the first turning on your right into a pedestrian precinct . At the next road junction turn left - Orchard Street - and right at the next - Union Road. Follow this for 1/4 mile to where it turns sharp right. Here a little to your left in Thorne Lock. Turn left and cross the canal bridge by the lock and turn left onto the path by the canal on your left. You now walk beside the canal for the next 2 miles. In 1/2 mile walk under the A614 road bridge; on the other side almost dwarfed by it is the Canal Tavern. On your right is the Rising Sun Inn.

Continue by the canal and in 3/4 mile pass a marina on the otherside of the canal. 1/4 mile later pass an impressive cantilever bridge.

Little over 1/4 mile later gain Moores Bridge. Here leave the canal and turn left over the bridge and cross the railway line just after. Shortly afterwards bear left along Moore Edge Road, passing the drive to Long Meadows Farm on your right and later Moorhouse. After this the road bears left with the drive to Causeway Farm on your right. Follow the road round and keep straight at the junction following Church Balk. On your right is a school and playing fields. All the time form the canal the church tower has acted as a useful guide. As you near it you can walk through the churchyard back to the car-park or continue along the road and turn left.

STAINFORTH & KEADBY CANAL AT THORNE.

**MOORES BRIDGE Nr. THORNE
- STAINFORTH & KEADBY CANAL.**

CROWLE CHURCH.

CROWLE - 4 MILES

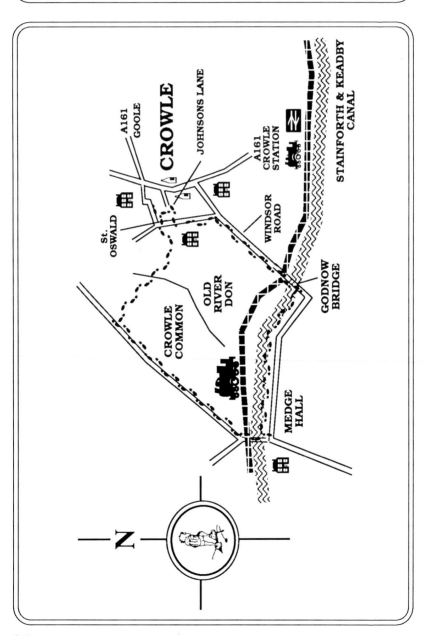

▪▪ ▪▪ - *Crowle - Old Don River - Crowle Common - Medge Hall - Stainforth & Keadby Canal - Godnow Bridge - Windsor - Crowle.*

 - *O.S. 1:50,000 Landranger Series, Sheet No. 112 - Scunthorpe.*

- *No official one but parking space on Church Street near St. Oswald's church.. Parking space close to canal near Medge Hall.*

- *Several near the Market Place in Crowle - George & Dragon, White Hart, Cross Keys, & Market Tavern.*

ABOUT THE WALK - Crowle is a very pleasant village and well worth exploring if time permits. The church is of particular interest with a Norman doorway and inside a 7th century cross shaft. The walk takes you through the village into the surrounding countryside to Medge Hall and the canal. Here you walk along the peaceful canal to Godnow Bridge, where you leave it and follow minor roads back to central Crowle and church where the walk began.

WALKING INSTRUCTIONS - Starting from the church dedicated to St. Oswald, walk along the narrow lane on its righthand side - between the houses - away from Church Street. After 200 yards and after passing Crowle Bowls Club on your left reach a road and turn left; opposite to your right is a chapel. Keep straight along the road to where it turns left. Here continue ahead onto a No Through Road - Marsh Road - which is bridlepath signed. Follow this for more than 1/4 mile to another bridlepath sign and turn right. Follow this track for little over 1/2 mile; keeping straight ahead all the time and crossing the Old Don River. After 1/2 mile reach a T junction of tracks and turn left. Follow this for a mile with a dike on your left to the railway and signal box at Medge Hall. Cross the railway line and bridge over the canal and turn left immediately to a gate and the track beside the canal on your left.

Keep to this track by the canal for a mile to a stile before Godnow Bridge. Turn left over the bridge and cross the railway again and walk along Windsor Road for 3/4 mile. Entering the houses of Windsor take the first road on your left. Keep on this road for 1/4 mile and take the second road on your right - Johnsons Lane. A little way along here turn left along Vicarage Walk and regain Church Street and St. Oswald's church.

**HISTORICAL SIGNS AT MEDGE HALL
-STAINFORTH & KEADBY CANAL.**

STAINFORTH & KEADBY CANAL AT MEDGE HALL.

STAINFORTH & KEADBY CANAL NEAR CROWLE.

KEADBY TO CROWLE STATION - 4 MILES

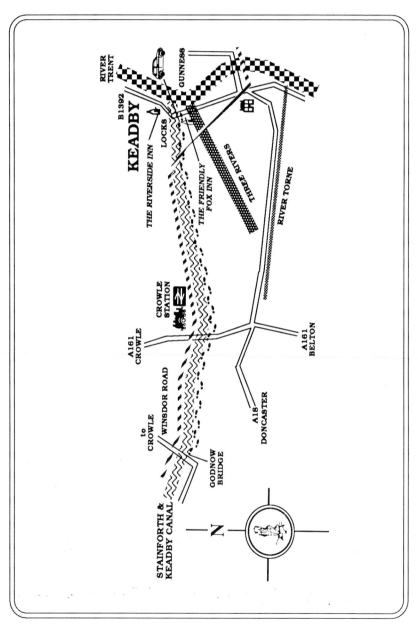

Keadby - Stainforth & Keadby Canal to Crowle Station. The walk can be extended to Godnow Bridge and joining the Crowle/ Medge Hall walk. This adds on an extra 1 1/2 miles - about 40 mins extra of walking.

- O.S. 1:50,000 Landranger Series, Sheet No. 112 - Scunthorpe,

- Beside canal down lane on righthand side of The Friendly Fox Inn at Keadby. Grid Ref. TA 834114.

- The Riverside Inn and The Friendly Fox Inn, Keadby.

- Several in Crowle 1 3/4 mile from Crowle Station, including George & Dragon, White Hart, Cross Keys and Market Tavern; all in the Market area.

ABOUT THE WALK - The principal aim of the walk is to see where the canal meets the River Trent. It is worth exploring Keadby to walk along the river bank to observe the ships that come here, as well as seeing the locks linking the canal to the river.

WALKING INSTRUCTIONS - This is basically a one-way walk to either Crowle Station or onto Godnow Bridge. The walking is flat and along a good towpath, popular with fishermen, on the lefthand side of the canal. There is nothing to stop you form doing an 8 mile or 11 mile return walk. It is a peaceful area and a great contrast in canal construction and setting to those in Nottinghamshire, Derbyshire, Staffordshire & Cheshire where it is often hilly country and much narrower canals.

SHEFFIELD & SOUTH YORKSHIRE NAVIGATION - END TO END - 43 MILES

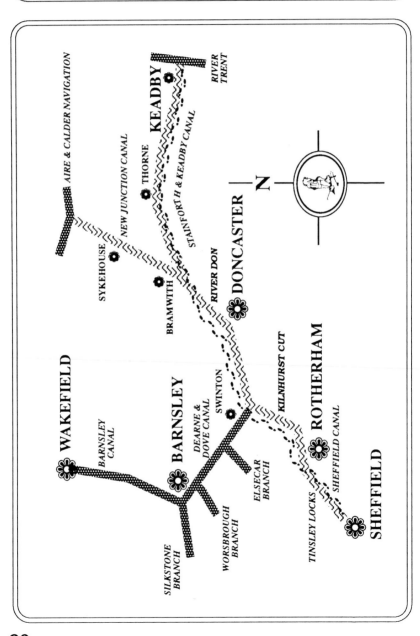

SHEFFIELD & SOUTH YORKSHIRE NAVIGATION - END TO END - 43 MILES (69 km)

 O.S. Landranger Series 1:50,000 Sheet Nos -

111 - Sheffield & Doncaster area.
112 - Scunthorpe

- Castle Basin, Sheffield - Sheffield Canal - Ickles Lock - Rotherham - River Don - Kilnhurst Cut - Mexborough Cut - River Don - Sprotborough Lock - Doncaster - River Don - Barnby Dun - Stainforth & Keadby Canal - Thorne - Keadby.

ABOUT THE WALK - For those wanting a two day/ weekend walk you can start from the Castle Basin area in Sheffield and walk along the canals and rivers to Keadby, where the canal meets the River Trent. The walk comprises of a canal at each end - Sheffield and the Stainforth & Keadby - with river section between Tinsley and Doncaster. Doncaster is half-way. Road walking will be necessary from Ickles Lock to the northern side of Rotherham; otherwise you will be by the water all the way.

Mileages -

Sheffield to Keadby - 43 miles
Sheffield to Rotherham - 6 1/2 miles
Rotherham to Doncaster - 15 miles
Doncaster to Keadby - 21 1/2 miles

Other permutations include -

1. Sheffield to Wakefield via Sheffield Canal, River Don, Dearne & Dove Canal and Barnsley Canal - about 30 miles.

2. Sheffield to Aire & Calder Navigation via Sheffield Canal, River Don and New Junction Canal - about 36 miles.

CANAL FEATURES - to look for

STOP PLANKS - *in various places can be seen vertical grooves in the canal walls - especially near bridges - with handled planks stacked nearby. The planks are slotted into the grooves sealing the canal while repairs or cleaning of the drained section is carried out.*

ROPE GROOVES - *on the side of bridges, sometimes with either cast iron or wooden shields, can be seen the grooves cut by the horse tow lines over the decades, such as the photograph below at Walton Bridge on the Barnsley Canal.*

TURNOVER/CROSSOVER BRIDGES - *in a few places the tow-path switches sides of the canal and a bridge was built to enable the horse to cross over without unhitching the line. The Macclesfield Canal has several splendid examples.*

SWING BRIDGES - *as the name implies, the bridge could be swung out of the way to allow boats to pass.*

BALANCED BRIDGES - *bridges finely balanced that can be either pushed upwards out of the way or lowered across the canal.*

SKEW BRIDGES - *most canal bridges are built at right angles to the canal. In a few cases to avoid the Z bend in the road the bridge was built at an angle.*

ROPE GROOVES AT WALTON BRIDGE, BARNSLEY CANAL.

CANAL MUSEUMS & OTHERS OF RELATED INTEREST.

1. The Canal and National Waterways Museum,
The Boat Museum,
Dockyard Road,
Ellesmere Port,
South Wirral.
L65 4EF
Tel. No 051-355 5017

2. British Waterways Board,
   Waterways Museum,
   Stoke Bruerne,
   Towcester,
   Northants.

3. The National Waterways Museum,
   Llanthony Warehouse,
   Gloucester Docks,
   Gloucester.
   GL1 2EH

   Tel. No. 0452-25524

OTHERS OF RELATED INTEREST -

4. Kelham Island Industrial Museum,
   Kelham Island,
   Sheffield.
   South Yorkshire.

5. Dearne Valley Country Park,
   Barnsley,
   South Yorkshire.

6. Elsecar Industrial Park & Greenway,
   Near Barnsley.
   South Yorkshire.

CANAL SOCIETIES & USEFUL ADDRESSES -

BRITISH WATERWAYS BOARD,
MELBURY HOUSE,
MELBURY TERRACE,
LONDON.
NW1 6JX
Tel. 081 - 262 6711

AIRE & CALDER NAVIGATION -
SOUTH YORKSHIRE BOAT CLUB,
MRS. S. SANDON,
25, WESTFIELD LANE,
EMLEY MOOR,
HUDDERSFIELD,
WEST YORKSHIRE.
Tel. 0924-840347

SHEFFIELD & SOUTH YORKSHIRE NAVIGATION -
SHEFFIELD CANAL ASSOCIATION,
B. MARTIN,
CANAL WHARF,
SHEFFIELD,
SOUTH YORKSHIRE.
S2

STRAWBERRY ISLAND BOAT CLUB,
P.HARBON,
C/O SIBC.,
MILETHORN LANE,
DONCASTER,
SOUTH YORKSHIRE.
Tel. 0302 - 64954

SUGGESTED FURTHER READING
- a Random selection.

"llustrations of Barnsley Canal Trails " M.L. Jefferson 1977.
"The Canals of Yorkshire & North East England "- 2 vols - Charles Hadfield - david & Charles 1972.
"The Early History of the Don Navigation" T.S.Willan Manchester University Press 1965
"Transport & Industruy in South Yorkshire " P.H.Abell 1977
"Memories of the Sheffield & South Yorkshire Navigation " Mike Taylor Yorkshire Waterways Publications 1988.
"British Canals - an Illustrated History" Charles Hadfield David & Charles 1979
"James Brindley" H. Bode Shlre Publictions 1973
Nicholson/Ordnance Survey Gulde to the Waterways - Vol 3 - North
"Discovering Canals in Britain" Peter L.Smith Shire Publications
"Discovering Lost Canals" Ronald Russell Shire Publications
"Inland Cruising" Tom Willis Pelham Books.

OTHER CANAL WALK BOOKS BY JOHN N. MERRILL

Vol 1 - Derbyshire and Nottinghamshire.
- more than 30 walks on the Chesterfield, Cromford, Erewash, Nutbrook, Derby, Nottingham and Trent & Mersey Canals.

Vol 2 - Cheshire and Staffordshire.
- More than 40 walks on the Peak Forest, Macclesfield, Caldon and Trent & Mersey canals.

VOL 3 - Staffordshire.
- More than 30 walks on the Trent & Mersey, Staffordshire & Worcestershlre, and Coventry canals.

Vol 6 - Walking the CHESHIRE RING.
- The 97 mile walk around the ring is one of finest canal walks in Britain. The Ashton, Rochdale, Bridgewater, Trent &Mersey, Macclesfield and Peak Forest Canals. Bokk details the walk in stages.

FORTHCOMING -
Vol 5 - Nottinghamshire, Leicestershire and Lincolnshire.
- deals with River Trent, Grantham Canal, River Soar, Witham Navigation, and Foss Dyke Navigation.

Vol 7 - The Trent & Mersey Canal
- end to end walk.

Vol 8 & 9 - Birmingham Canals - North & South

KEADBY LOCK.

RIVER TRENT AT KEADBY.

WALK RECORD CHART

Date Walked

THE SHEFFIELD CANAL -
SHEFFIELD TO ROTHERHAM - 7 MILES ....
RIVER DON NAVIGATION -
KILNHURST CUT - 6 MILES..
MEXBOROUGH NEW CUT - 4 MILES ....
SPROTBROUGH & CONISBROUGH CASTLE
- 3 WALKS...
SPROTBROUGH & CUSWORTH HALL
- 7 MILES ....
THE DEARNE & DOVE CANAL -
SWINTON LOCKS TO ELSECAR BRANCH - 5 MILES........
ELSECAR & WORSBROUGH BRANCHES - 13 MILES.......
THE BARNSLEY CANAL -
CENTRAL BARNSLEY - 2 MILES.....................................
DEARNE VALLEY PARK - 4 MILES..................................
SILKSTONE BRANCH - 2,5,&7 MILES.............................
ROYSTON - 3 MILES ....
HAW PARK - 4 MILES ....
RIVER DUN NAVIGATION -
ARKSEY & BENTLEY COMMON - 5 MILES......................
NEW JUNCTION CANAL -
BRAITHWAITE & BRAMWITH - 4 MILES.........................
SYKEHOUSE - 7 1/2 MILES ....
STAINFORTH & KEADBY CANAL -
THORNE - WEST - 8 MILES ....
THORNE - EAST - 4 MILES..
CROWLE - 4 MILES..
KEADBY TO CROWLE STATION - 4 MILES.....................
SHEFFIELD & SOUTH YORKSHIRE
NAVIGATION - END TO END - 43 MILES ....

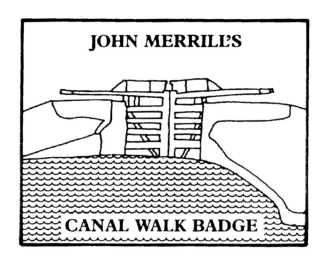

JOHN MERRILL'S

CANAL WALK BADGE

EQUIPMENT NOTES
- Some personal thoughts

BOOTS - *preferably with a full leather upper, of medium weight, with a vibram sole. I always add a foam cushioned insole to help cushion the base of my feet.*

SOCKS - *I generally wear two thick pairs as this helps minimise blisters. The inner pair are of loop stitch variety and approximately 80% wool. The outer are a thick rib pair of approximately 80% wool.*

WATERPROOFS - *for general walking I wear a T shirt or cotton shirt with a cotton wind jacket on top. You generate heat as you walk and I prefer to layer my clothes to avoid getting too hot. Depending on the season will dictate how many layers you wear. In soft rain I just use my wind jacket for I know it quickly dries out. In heavy or consistant rain I slip on a neoprene lined gagoule, and although hot and clammy it does keep me reasonably dry. Only in extreme conditions will I don overtrousers, much preferring to get wet and feel comfortable. I never wear gaiters!*

FOOD - *as I walk I carry bars of chocolate, for they provide instant energy and are light to carry. In winter a flask of hot coffee is welcome. I never carry water and find no hardship from not doing so, but this is a personal matter! From experience I find the more I drink the more I want and sweat. You should always carry some extra food such as Kendal Mint Cake, for emergencies.*

RUCKSACKS - *for day walking I use a climbing rucksack of about 40 litre capacity and although it leaves excess space it does mean that the sac is well padded, with an internal frame and padded shoulder straps. Inside apart from the basics for one day I carry gloves, balaclava, spare pullover and a pair of socks.*

MAP & COMPASS - *when I am walking I always have the relevant map - preferably 1:25,000 scale - open in my hand. This enables me to constantly check that I am walking the right way. In case of bad weather I carry a compass, which once mastered gives you complete confidence in thick cloud or mist.*

REMEMBER AND
OBSERVE
THE COUNTRY CODE

 Enjoy the countryside and respect its life and work.

 Guard against all risk of fire.

 Fasten all gates.

 Keep your dogs under close control.

 Keep to public paths across farmland.

 Use gates and stiles to cross fences, hedges and walls.

 Leave livestock, crops and machinery alone.

 Take your litter home - pack it in; pack it out.

Help to keep all water clean.

 Protect wildlife, plants and trees.

Take special care on country roads.

THE HIKER'S CODE

✿ *Hike only along marked routes - do not leave the trail.*

✿ *Use stiles to climb fences; close gates.*

✿ *Camp only in designated campsites.*

✿ *Carry a light-weight stove.*

✿ *Leave the trail cleaner than you found it.*

✿ *Leave flowers and plants for others to enjoy.*

✿ *Keep dogs on a leash.*

✿ *Protect and do not disturb wildlife.*

✿ *Use the trail at your own risk.*

✿ *Leave only your thanks and footprints - take nothing but photographs.*

OTHER BOOKS by
JOHN N. MERRILL
PUBLISHED by
JNM PUBLICATIONS

CIRCULAR WALK GUIDES -
SHORT CIRCULAR WALKS IN THE PEAK DISTRICT
LONG CIRCULAR WALKS IN THE PEAK DISTRICT
CIRCULAR WALKS IN WESTERN PEAKLAND
SHORT CIRCULAR WALKS IN THE STAFFORDSHIRE MOORLANDS
SHORT CIRCULAR WALKS AROUND THE TOWNS & VILLAGES OF
THE PEAK DISTRICT
SHORT CIRCULAR WALKS AROUND MATLOCK
SHORT CIRCULAR WALKS IN THE DUKERIES
SHORT CIRCULAR WALKS IN SOUTH YORKSHIRE
SHORT CIRCULAR WALKS IN SOUTH DERBYSHIRE
SHORT CIRCULAR WALKS AROUND BUXTON
SHORT CIRCULAR WALKS IN THE HOPE VALLEY
40 SHORT CIRCULAR WALKS IN THE PEAK DISTRICT
CIRCULAR WALKS ON KINDER & BLEAKLOW
SHORT CIRCULAR WALKS IN SOUTH NOTTINGHAMSHIRE
SHIRT CIRCULAR WALKS IN CHESHIRE
SHORT CIRCULAR WALKS IN WEST YORKSHIRE

CANAL WALKS -
VOL 1 - DERBYSHIRE & NOTTINGHAMSHIRE
VOL 2 - CHESHIRE & STAFFORDSHIRE
VOL 3 - STAFFORDSHIRE
VOL 4 - THE CHESHIRE RING
VOL 5 - LINCOLNSHIRE & NOTTINGHAMSHIRE
VOL 6 - SOUTH YORKSHIRE
VOL 7 - THE TRENT & MERSEY CANAL

JOHN MERRILL DAY CHALLENGE WALKS -
WHITE PEAK CHALLENGE WALK
DARK PEAK CHALLENGE WALK
PEAK DISTRICT END TO END WALKS
STAFFORDSHIRE MOORLANDS CHALLENGE WALK
THE LITTLE JOHN CHALLENGE WALK
YORKSHIRE DALES CHALLENGE WALK
NORTH YORKSHIRE MOORS CHALLENGE WALK
LAKELAND CHALLENGE WALK
THE RUTLAND WATER CHALLENGE WALK
INSTRUCTION & RECORD -
HIKE TO BE FIT.....STROLLING WITH JOHN
THE JOHN MERRILL WALK RECORD BOOK

MULTIPLE DAY WALKS -
THE RIVERS'S WAY
PEAK DISTRICT: HIGH LEVEL ROUTE
PEAK DISTRICT MARATHONS
THE LIMEY WAY
THE PEAKLAND WAY

COAST WALKS & NATIONAL TRAILS -
ISLE OF WIGHT COAST PATH
PEMBROKESHIRE COAST PATH
THE CLEVELAND WAY

PEAK DISTRICT HISTORICAL GUIDES -
A to Z GUIDE OF THE PEAK DISTRICT
DERBYSHIRE INNS - an A to Z guide
HALLS AND CASTLES OF THE PEAK DISTRICT & DERBYSHIRE
TOURING THE PEAK DISTRICT & DERBYSHIRE BY CAR
DERBYSHIRE FOLKLORE
PUNISHMENT IN DERBYSHIRE
CUSTOMS OF THE PEAK DISTRICT & DERBYSHIRE
WINSTER - a souvenir guide
ARKWRIGHT OF CROMFORD
TALES FROM THE MINES by Geoffrey Carr
PEAK DISTRICT PLACE NAMES by Martin Spray

JOHN MERRILL'S MAJOR WALKS -
TURN RIGHT AT LAND'S END
WITH MUSTARD ON MY BACK
TURN RIGHT AT DEATH VALLEY
EMERALD COAST WALK

COLOUR GUIDES -
THE PEAK DISTRICT.........Something to remember her by.

SKETCH BOOKS -
NORTH STAFFORDSHIRE SKETCHBOOK by John Creber
SKETCHES OF THE PEAK DISTRICT

IN PREPARATION -
LONG CIRCULAR WALKS IN STAFFORDSHIRE
SHORT CIRCULAR WALKS IN THE YORKSHIRE DALES
SHORT CIRCULAR WALKS IN THE LAKE DISTRICT
SHORT CIRCULAR WALKS IN NORTH YORKSHIRE MOORS
SNOWDONIA CHALLENGE WALK
FOOTPATHS OF THE WORLD - Vol 1 - NORTH AMERICA
HIKING IN NEW MEXICO

☞ **Full list from JNM PUBLICATIONS, Winster, Matlock, Derbys.**

SHEFFIELD CANAL AT ATTERCLIFFE.

STAINFORTH & KEADBY CANAL AT KEADBY.